STRANGER
in the
MIDST

STRANGER
in the
MIDST

A Memoir
of Spiritual
Discovery

Nan Fink

BasicBooks
A Division of HarperCollinsPublishers

Grateful acknowledgment is made for permission to reprint from the following: The second stanza of "Lemon Sponge," by Shirley Kaufman, from her *Rivers of Salt* (Port Townsend, WA: Copper Canyon Press, 1993).

Parts of this book have appeared in different versions in "A Question of Belonging," *Bridges*, vol. 3, no. 2 (1993) and "Crossing the Ethnic Divide: A Meditation on Anti-Semitism," *Tikkun*, vol. 10, no. 2 (1995).

Published by BasicBooks,
A Division of HarperCollins Publishers, Inc.

FIRST EDITION

Designed by Nancy Sabato

Library of Congress Cataloging-in-Publication Data

Fink, Nan.
    Stranger in the midst : a memoir of spiritual discovery / by Nan Fink.
        p. cm.
    ISBN 0-465-08200-9
    1. Fink, Nan.   2. Proselytes and proselytizing. Jewish—Converts from Christianity—Biography.   3. Jewish women —United States—Biography.   4. Jews—United States—Biography.   I. Title.
BM729.P7F56   1997
296.7'14'092—dc21
[B]   96-46249

97 98 99 00 01 ❖/RRD 10 9 8 7 6 5 4 3 2 1

To My Children

What lets us be who we most are?
Suppose we only had to know
the climate, what grows where,
how rich or shallow the soil is.
A kind of field guide
for dislocated souls:
how to be rooted, how to be
born in an ancient cycle
from seed to seed,
dust of our old selves settling
over a new season.

Shirley Kaufman, 1993

Acknowledgments

Many people contributed to this memoir's publication and helped to shape the way it was written. With deep gratitude I thank the following:

Elizabeth Kaplan, my agent, whose belief in the book made it a reality.

Jo Ann Miller, formerly of Basic Books, and Susan Rabiner, editorial director of Basic Books, who oversaw the publishing of this book.

Juliana Nocker, associate editor of Basic Books, who guided me through the editorial process, and Richard Fumosa, project editor, who supervised the book's production.

Esther Broner, for encouraging me to write this book as a memoir.

Susan Griffin, for her useful suggestions in the early stages of conceptualizing the material.

Julie Chagi, Mari Coates, Connie Matthiessen, Linda Moyer, and Lynn Sydney, the members of my writing group, for their invaluable insights and ideas.

Shoshana Alexander, Sandra Butler, Joan Cole, Marcia Freedman, Michelle Holstein, Jonathan Omer-Man, and Lisa Piediscalzi for their careful reading of the manuscript and their helpful editorial suggestions.

Rachel Cowan, Avram Davis, Burt Jacobson, Michael Lerner, Zalman Schachter-Shalomi, Susie Schneider, David Wolfe-Blank, and David Zeller for their help in exploring the meaning of conversion.

Those converts who spoke freely and at length to me about their experience.

Kirk Allen, Jane Ariel, Barry Barkan, Barbara Bernstein, Stanley Bernstein, Sandy Boucher, Jeri Cohen, Marinell Eva, Abigail Grafton, Bill Holstein, Jacqueline Holstein, Sarah Holstein, Donna Karones, Shirley Kaufman, Vera Long, Nick Piediscalzi, Arlene Schmaeff, Marion Souyoultzis, Zafiris Souyoultzis, Linda Wilson, and my students at Chochmat HaLev for their continued support.

Jonathan, whose wise presence sustained me in the months of writing.

My children, who continued to teach me about kindness and honesty during the process.

The members of my family and my partners, for their generosity in allowing their personal lives to be revealed in these pages.

Introduction

Passover, 1995

I have returned to Jerusalem, the city that is my touch-stone. Here I reach a level of honesty that is hard to find in the more diffuse atmosphere of California, where I live. Jerusalem does not let me escape myself. My tears at the Western Wall are only the beginning.

I have come for a month to write, but I want nothing more than to sit by my apartment window. The pale spring sky, the pitted stone buildings, the streets of the Old City remind me of the past. I cannot forget my excitement and love, my anger and disillusionment, and my efforts at reconciliation.

When I first visited Jerusalem a decade ago, I was not yet a Jew. Unsure of myself, I walked these same city streets knowing that I was different from those around me but believing that once I converted it would not matter. I dreamed of finding a place among this people I loved.

If anyone had asked me why I was converting, I could not have answered. My life was filled with too many contradictions. I who was born into a Christian family, and was once married to a Protestant minister, had a deep longing to be a Jew. This desire had grown steadily through the years, so that by the time I reached Jerusalem, I was consumed by it.

Later I would understand that my decision to change religions came from experiences as diverse as exploring the creek by my childhood home and participating in Vietnam

War protests with my secular Jewish friends. The journey to Judaism was neither logical nor linear.

When I converted, I did not anticipate the struggle to be accepted as a Jew. The Jewish community, as I know it, is ambivalent toward its converts and suspicious of our motives. It often treats us as unwanted visitors. To protect myself against this rejection, I sometimes concealed my Gentile background.

I have learned from my conversations with dozens of converts that this deception is not unusual. Many of us make ourselves invisible, like the salt religious Jews sprinkle on challah on Shabbat. But this attempt to fit in separates us from our life's experience, and we bear the burden of dishonesty.

The Jewish community often questions the legitimacy of converts, but we are not alone. Jews in interfaith relationships, unaffiliated Jews, gay and lesbian Jews, African-American and Asian Jews, and even unmarried Jews are treated similarly. We are pushed to the margins of the community because we threaten its cohesiveness.

Conversion raises the issue of identity. When I crossed the ethnic divide, I was forced to examine myself in ways I had avoided. Sometimes I did not know who I was. No longer a Christian but insecure as a Jew, I felt disoriented and confused.

Even my vision changed after conversion. Experiencing anti-Semitism, I began to see the world through a Jewish lens. But my children are not Jewish, nor is my family of origin, and I feared that this change in me would hurt our connection. My loyalty was split between the people I was joining and those closest to me. At times I felt I was being pulled apart.

I also struggled with Judaism itself. When I converted, I thought I had found a spiritual home, but I soon realized that I could not accept the religion in its most traditional form. As a woman, I felt excluded. My search for a more meaningful spirituality within Judaism took me through periods of intense frustration and discouragement until I reached a deeper understanding.

The past decade has been filled with upheaval. I've experienced the making and breaking of a marriage and a partnership, the creation of *Tikkun* magazine, the involvement in Jewish politics, the reworking of relationships in my family, the drawing into the self, and the spiritual reemergence.

I'd like to believe that the most wrenching part of becoming a Jew is over. Certainly I am more secure in my identity. I've deepened spiritually, finding a way to observe Judaism that fulfills me. But the crowd milling in the Old City street below reminds me that nothing stays put. Permanence is an illusion.

A white dove flies close by my apartment window, circling and returning. I watch as it settles on the railing of my balcony, gently fluffing its wings. The sight is so perfect it hardly seems real. An omen. Even though my life will continue to change, the dove gives me hope that it will be accompanied by a greater feeling of integration.

In the end, my journey has been one of self-realization. Like others who make great life changes, I have come to know and live by my own truth. Despite the many mistakes made along the way, despite the doubt, despite the difficulty, I have arrived where I want to be.

Ten years ago, five years, even one year ago, I was not ready to write about this journey. I did not have enough distance. But now the words well up within me and I want to let them go, so that the truth of my experience will be known.

Only a few converts to Judaism have written about their lives. They take the reader with them to the *mikveh*, the pool of water where they immerse and become Jews, but seldom do they go further in describing their experience. Their stories are positive throughout, perhaps true for some converts but not for most, as I've learned.

There is another story to tell. This one is far stormier, fraught with ambiguities and vacillations. It speaks of the pain of changing identities and balancing loyalties. It describes spiritual disillusionment, as well as the love of Judaism.

In many ways my story is universal. Those of us who make major life changes share the experience of leaving behind one world and moving into another. We both lose and gain. This is true whether we embrace a new religion, or acknowledge a different sexual orientation, or radically change our lifestyle. Courage sometimes fails, yet the imperative to become more fully ourselves remains. We know what we must do.

My story is set in a context of Jewish concerns. I cannot describe my spiritual journey without including my relationship to the Jewish community. The question of who is considered a Jew and the confusion about the conversion process shaped my search for meaning, just as the stories I heard from other converts informed my understanding.

Converts to Judaism are strangers in the midst of a people bound by blood and history. In the United States alone, our number is now over 200,000. My hope is that my story will familiarize others with our experience. So little is known. We are seldom asked questions, for fear of embarrassing us, and we seldom speak about ourselves, for fear of appearing different.

But ignorance about converts causes pain. The world we've left behind does not understand us. And as strangers in the Jewish community, we've often been misunderstood and mistreated, our contributions discounted.

As I think of these things, my breath quickens. There is so much. But the breeze rustles through my window, and the golden dome on the Temple Mount in the distance catches my eye. The white dove spreads its wings, ready to take off for another balcony. This city, with its beauty, astounds me. It gives me the strength to begin.

I remember my first Jerusalem window, rolled halfway down in the back of the *sherut,* the shared taxi that carried me along the streets of the city. It was Friday evening, ten years ago. I had just arrived from the United States.

Squeezed among the other passengers, I strained to get a glimpse of Jerusalem out the window. Everywhere I saw stone. Stone buildings, stone walls, stone pathways, all glowing with a soft yellow light. The desert air coming through the window was warm and fragrant. The streets were empty. A great hush had fallen on the city in these last remaining moments of sunlight.

"It's not Shabbat yet, is it?" I asked the English-speaking woman next to me.

"You'll make it to the hotel before the siren," she answered.

"Good," I nodded, pleased. I knew about the Jerusalem siren from Michael, my lover. He had told me that it is sounded each Friday at sundown to mark the beginning of the Sabbath, and that I would arrive in time for it, assuming my plane wasn't late.

The driver dropped me off in front of my hotel just as the sun dipped over the edge of the city. As I entered the lobby, I heard a deep, unmistakable sound. I stopped to listen, feeling the siren's tone reverberate through my travel-weary body. Shabbat had arrived in all its glory, and I felt as if I had reached the center of the universe.

The Shabbat siren was only the first discovery of that

visit to Jerusalem. The whole summer would be marked by such sweetness. Subsequent trips to Israel were more difficult, even horrific, but in those few months, before I became a Jew, I was like a child, open and receptive to everything. Truth seemed to abide in the stone streets, the mountain air, the hot sun.

I was in a state of suspension in those days, learning about the tradition without making judgments. Later I would question everything I had absorbed, but that summer I cared more about becoming familiar with the details of Jewish life than rejecting them.

My imagination was inflamed. When I heard a lecture one evening about not wearing leather on the day of Tisha b'Av because it is a time of mourning, I dreamed about the people through history who walked these Jerusalem streets in porous shoes, feeling the stones sharp underfoot, weeping from the loss of Jewish life I was just beginning to understand.

That summer I was relieved to be away from California. When I went to the Western Wall, as I often did, I sank into despair about the life I had left behind. It was more tangled than I ever intended, and I could not figure out how to set it straight.

A year before, in 1984, I had moved from the Midwest back to California, the state of my birth. Since then, the familiar markers of self had slipped away: I had gone through a painful separation from my husband of eleven years, my youngest child left for college, and my career as a psychotherapist and teacher was on hold until I decided what to do next. The enormous responsibilities of family and profession that I had carried over the previous two decades no longer existed.

A great space had opened up, and it was being filled

with something that had been left undone too long: I was studying to become a Jew.

Although I knew about Jewish culture from my close relationship to secular Jews, I had a lot to learn about the religion itself. I had been spiritually drawn to it for years. Even before I left the Midwest, I thought I would convert, but I hadn't had the time to study it in depth. Now I learned Hebrew at night school, and read books about Jewish prayer, and immersed myself in Jewish history and philosophy.

I was intoxicated by my studies, but other parts of my life were not going well. My effort to convert was creating a distance between my three children and me. Even though they were in college and out on their own, considered adult, this decision greatly affected them.

I was moving away from them, into a place they could not go unless they also converted. They did their best to support me, but I worried that they were being hurt. They were familiar with Judaism, as they had gone to a Jewish nursery school when they were young, and we had celebrated Jewish holidays with friends. But I had existed with them on the Gentile side of the ethnic line, and now I was crossing over, leaving them behind.

Other members of my family were not pleased by what I was doing. My mother, who lives not far from me, had hoped that once I moved back to California I would come to her church. But instead, I attended Jewish services and was careful about what I ate, turning down her offers of nonkosher meat and seafood, filling my plate with vegetables and fruit. What had happened to me?

Even worse, I had fallen in love with Michael. His great passion for Judaism and his whirlwind energy and incisive mind had attracted me from the moment I met him.

We were living together in his house nestled among the oak trees, with its kosher kitchen and strict observance of Shabbat. This experience of Jewish living was a pleasure, and important because I wanted to explore it, but it made my family uncomfortable.

"I can't call you on Saturdays?" my daughter asked. It was confusing enough that I was now in another relationship, but this new way of life made it harder to accept.

"I'm so sorry," I answered guiltily. "We don't answer the phone on Shabbat."

I was also having a difficult time in the orthodox shul, where I had been going to services with Michael and his teenage son for the last few months. Although I had hoped to find friends in this new community, hardly anyone would speak to me. It was not my imagination. One day an anonymous letter arrived, scrawled on light blue notepaper, telling me that I didn't belong at the shul. Shocked, I quickly tore the letter to shreds.

This was only a preview of what would come. A few weeks later one of the woman congregants beckoned me to the side of the room after the service. I had seen her before, but we hadn't spoken. "Nobody wants you here," she said in a stern voice. "People are too polite to tell you directly, but that's how they feel. You're not welcome. Do you understand?"

I left the shul weeping, and walked around the block until it was time to drive back to the house. "What happened?" Michael asked, when he saw my tear-stained face.

"I'm being shunned," I replied.

He reassured me that this woman was one of the most unsociable members of the congregation, and that she surely didn't speak for everyone. "I know it's hard, but just hang in," he said. "It'll take a little while, but they'll probably end up liking you better than they like me."

I laughed at the idea, but I couldn't stop thinking about the hostility that had been directed at me. Was it because I was a Gentile? The orthodox community was small and ingrown, and I came from a world considered threatening by many of them. But I also knew that the Torah, the five books of Moses, was clear in its instructions to Jews to be kind to the stranger in their midst. One of the congregants had even given a *drash,* a sermon, on that subject recently.

The problem more likely had to do with my connection to Michael. He had recently broken off a relationship with a woman highly regarded in the congregation, and the sympathy of the people was with her. I was the interloper, the seductive *shiksa,* the non-Jewish stranger who had come in and stolen a Jewish heart.

The idea of being seen in this light disturbed me, as I hadn't thought I was taking away another woman's man. Still, I could understand the pain of a failed relationship, and I knew what it was like to take the side of someone who had been rejected. After much consideration I decided I would continue going to the shul, with the hope that this matter of the heart would soon be resolved.

But the wrath of the congregation was not easily assuaged. Someone managed to find out that I was studying for conversion with a rabbi from a local conservative synagogue. I had chosen this man because the orthodox shul did not have a rabbi of its own. The conservative rabbi, new in town, could not have been prepared for the harassment he received on my account. First came nasty letters, then he was awakened in the middle of the night by anonymous telephone callers, telling him in disguised voices that he shouldn't convert me.

I had stumbled into a community unlike any I had known. Never had I experienced such rejection and disrespect. As painful as this was, I was saved from total discouragement by hardly believing it was happening. How could these people act this way toward me when they didn't even know me? I became stubborn, and determined to stick it through. I would not let myself get drummed out of this congregation.

Looking back, I am amazed that I continued coming to services. The slightest hint of ambivalence, much less rejection, is usually enough to make me retreat. But I was building a life with Michael, and I didn't want him and his son to lose their connection to the congregation on my account.

Besides, I wanted certain things for myself from this orthodox shul. I loved the little building, with its simple white walls and big windows, and the wood ark holding the Torah at the front of the room. Even the division of the men and women seemed beautiful at that time. I'd see Michael on the other side of the *mehitzah,* the four-foot barrier that separated the sexes, and admire his curly hair, full beard, and intense gray eyes. We'd exchange smiles. Male and female energy, separate, made all the more potent by the separation.

I was moved by the way everyone sang the prayers together. Even though I knew only a little Hebrew, I soon was singing the haunting melodies, mouthing the unfamiliar syllables and sounds. Three hours of this on Saturday mornings, with the sunlight streaming into the room through the open windows and the chairs shuffling around me, put me into a deeply meditative state, one I had never experienced in any other religious service. When the congregation became silent during the *Amidah,* the most personal prayer, I felt connected to the source of all life, and connected to the community at the same time. I was exhilarated.

Inexplicably I had arrived at this little shul. The congregants might not approve of me, and I wasn't sure about them, but my spiritual journey had brought me here. After many years as an atheist, then awakening to the spiritual dimension of life, I yearned to be part of a religious community. I had been lonely too long.

The shul was also a good place for me to continue learning about Judaism, with its classes and Torah study sessions. I'd sit on the far side of the room, hardly saying a word, dreaming over this or that new piece of knowledge. It seemed important to absorb as much as I could.

I am surprised that my decision to convert was not affected by the people at the shul. But the decision had been made before I met them. Besides, I had known and loved too many Jews, and had too much experience in the Jewish community to think that these people represented all of orthodox life, much less all of Jewish life. And I was too angry at them to let them have power over my decision.

Just when the difficulties with my children and the orthodox shul seemed to reach their peak, Michael and I decided to go to Jerusalem. I was emotionally spent from all that had happened in the past year, and the idea of taking a leave of absence from my problems appealed to me. There would be time later on to sort everything through.

With great relief, then, I arrived alone in Jerusalem on that Friday evening in 1985, with Michael scheduled to come ten days later. After listening to the Shabbat siren, I hurriedly checked into the hotel and climbed the stairs to my third-floor room. Throwing open the doors to the veranda, breathing in the air that now had a hint of coolness, I watched the streets below fill as people came out of their apartments in ones and twos, on their way to evening services. I would follow them, I decided. And so on my first night in Jerusalem, I ended up at a Shabbat service, singing "*L'Cha Dodi*" and the other familiar songs with the congregation, comfortably anonymous in the women's balcony. I could hardly believe I had made it that far.

After Shabbat was over, on Sunday morning, I lugged my suitcase to the nearby apartment that Michael and I had rented for the summer. Furnished with a sagging bed, a table, and a few broken chairs, it lacked the charm I had imagined, but it would have to do. Later I'd buy some flowers and fix it up. But for now I had a very important task. I needed to make contact right away with an orthodox rabbi whose name I had been given in California.

At my final session with the conservative rabbi before I left the States, he had surprised me by saying that he thought I was ready for conversion. Excitedly he explained his plan. He knew of an orthodox rabbi in Jerusalem who might do the job, and I should go to him immediately, once I arrived.

"Just imagine, becoming a Jew in *Eretz Israel*," he enthused. Perhaps he was relieved to pass me on to someone else after all the trouble I had caused, but I didn't care. The end of my conversion process seemed to be in sight. I could hardly wait.

That morning in Jerusalem I locked the apartment door and set out to find the orthodox rabbi at a yeshivah, a Jewish religious school, in the Old City. Jerusalem, with its winding streets, confused me, and I lost my way. Finally I wandered through what seemed to be the right gate, into a dark inner courtyard, where I was immediately approached by a black-suited young man. "What do you want?" he asked, eyeing me suspiciously.

"I'm looking for the rabbi," I answered. I showed him the letter of introduction the conservative rabbi had written for me in California, saying that, "This is not an ordinary candidate for conversion. She has studied Judaism for many years, and is an intelligent, warm, and caring individual with unquestionable motivation. This woman is ready to take on the yoke of heaven."

The enthusiastic recommendation of the conservative rabbi pleased me, even though he exaggerated the length of my serious Jewish study. I was especially impressed with his final mystical allusion to conversion, and hoped it would help slide me through the scrutiny of this new rabbi.

The man glanced at the letter, then led me to a small room off the courtyard, telling me to wait. After a while a woman with lively blue eyes and an air of authority came through the door and introduced herself. Dressed in the orthodox style, with long sleeves and stockings and her head covered, she shook my hand with a firm grasp. She was the rebbetzin, the wife of the rabbi and the mother of their fourteen children.

For the next forty minutes the rebbetzin proceeded to grill me about my past and my current life. Was I planning a marriage in the near future? No, I answered, since the issue of marriage had not been resolved between Michael and me. How was I supporting my children, two of whom were in college? I had inherited some money, I explained. But aren't the expenses really high? Yes, I answered, it's hard, but my children also contribute.

These were not the questions I had expected, and I squirmed with their invasiveness, but to my relief she seemed to accept my desire to convert. After checking to make sure that I knew how to keep a kosher kitchen and that I understood the details about observing Shabbat, she told me to wait.

Soon I was ushered in to see the rabbi, a man with a

silver beard trailing down to his chest and a black *kepah* on his head. He nodded to me in a businesslike way as I sat down at his table. I knew enough to nod back rather than extend my hand in greeting, as ultraorthodox men don't touch women other than their wives and daughters.

"So you want to convert?" he said. When I replied that I did, he asked me many of the same questions I had already answered. After a while, he grew silent, stroking his beard in long sweeps. "Come and live here, and by the end of next summer you'll be a Jew," he finally proclaimed.

I sat up straight. "A year?" I asked. "Why so long?" I explained that the rabbi in California had thought I was ready now, since I had been preparing intensively for quite some time.

He brushed my comments aside. "Now, a year, ten years later. What does it matter? You'll study with the rebbetzin. She teaches the women. And who knows? Since you're single, maybe there will be a *shidduch*. A lot of men here are looking for wives."

The rabbi's vision of my future was not at all what I had in mind, but I let him continue. "God becomes impatient when you come close to perfection," he warned. "Becoming a Jew is hard when you have one foot in one world and one in another." This, it appeared, was his rationale for me uprooting myself and moving to Israel.

"It's a big decision," I replied.

"Since you're trained as a psychotherapist, you'd be useful here," he continued. "Some of our people at the yeshivah could benefit from your help."

I nodded to show that I was open to the possibility. The rabbi paused for a minute. "I understand you have children in college, and tuition expenses," he said. "Therefore the conversion will cost only $8,000, a real bargain."

"What?" I could hardly believe what I was hearing. Converts sometimes pay a small amount for their rabbi's time over the course of conversion, but never money like this.

"Of course, you'll have the expense of living in Jerusalem and payment for the classes with the rebbetzin, and you'll need to make a financial contribution to the yeshivah."

"I see," I answered cooly.

"We won't talk about it again," the rabbi said. "You can give me a check, and nobody needs to know."

A sick feeling was flooding through me by then. My conversion was high and holy to me, the end point of a long spiritual search, and I didn't want it tainted by an under-the-table deal. "I'll consider it," I said.

"Good," he replied. "Don't let the length of time deter you. It will go by quickly."

As I rose to leave, the rebbetzin popped her head into her husband's study. "You've had your talk with the rabbi? Come with me."

She was on her way to teach a class, arms piled with books. Although I didn't want to have anything more to do with this yeshivah, I was curious to see who her students were and how she taught, so I followed her through the Old City streets until we came to the building where the women's classes were held. Inside a dark room three students quietly waited.

The rebbetzin began to talk to them about the commandment in the Torah to not covet your neighbor's wife. "Even though it sounds like it's meant just for men, it's important for us, too," she said. "Why do you think this is so?"

From my experience at Hebrew class and the Torah discussion group at the orthodox shul in California, I expected the class to be lively, but the rebbetzin could not get the subject off the ground. I was in no mood to say anything after my experience with the rabbi, and the other women shifted uncomfortably in their chairs.

Finally one woman began to speak. On and on she went, and after several minutes of trying to understand her point, I gave up. Her odd scrambling of words and her habit of looking at the ceiling while she talked made me guess that she would be among the people the rabbi had targeted for my therapeutic help, if I were to sign up with him.

"Very good, Karen," the rebbetzin said kindly, when she had finished. The class limped along for another fifteen minutes, with the rebbetzin discussing how it poisons a person's soul to want something that belongs to someone else.

When the session was over, I walked back to the yeshivah with the rebbetzin. "That girl who spoke in class never said a word before," she explained. "She comes from a troubled background."

"Do you have a lot of students like that?"

"Some are, some aren't." With that, she shook my hand cordially and we parted.

When I got back to my apartment that afternoon, I considered what had happened at the yeshivah. I was still fuming about the rabbi's request for money under the table. Surely conversion wasn't something to be paid for, like a new car.

Looking around the threadbare apartment, with its dirty linoleum floor and its streaked windows, I felt discouraged and very much alone. Converting was proving to be far more difficult than I had expected. First there had been the trouble at the orthodox shul in California, and now this.

Still, the experience at the yeshivah was funny, I had to admit. Who would have thought that I, the offspring of a long line of Protestants, would end up at that place. Later I learned that many wealthy American Jews send their grown children to the yeshivah as a last resort, believing that religious zeal is better than drugs or dysfunctional lives. The rabbi and rebbetzin have helped straighten out many disturbed people through the years. In the end I couldn't really condemn them for trying to find money wherever they could, with the yeshivah to support and fourteen children to raise.

At the time, however, I felt only disappointment. I had been infused with the conservative rabbi's dream of converting in Israel, but now, after this fiasco, it did not seem possible. I had no other leads. I later found out that I couldn't have converted in Israel anyhow unless I went through the official channels of the central Rabbinic Court. Studying with the rebbetzin at the orthodox rabbi's yeshivah would have been just the prelude to this other process, which could have taken years.

The summer stretched ahead of me, time to fill with whatever I wished. Determined that my disappointment about the orthodox rabbi not ruin my stay, I shelved the idea of conversion until I returned to the States. I would investigate other possibilities for the summer.

I had thought that yeshivah study in Israel was limited to men, but I soon learned from a few telephone calls of the existence of yeshivahs for women. The idea of intense study appealed to me. Michael would be busy all summer organizing a program in peace studies for the following year, and I wanted some kind of structure.

Carefully checking out the available programs, making sure I didn't get involved with a program like the orthodox rabbi's, I signed up at Mikhlelet Bruria, a modern orthodox yeshivah for women. With a day school on the first floor for the children of more advanced students, and several classes in Hebrew and English going on at the same time, the building had an air of purpose that I liked.

Every morning I'd take the bus, then climb the hill past the apartment buildings and the little park to this yeshivah for classes. There I'd listen as one teacher and then another spoke. Each day we had different subjects. Recently I found my notes from these classes: lists of rules for observing Shabbat, guidelines for Jewish holidays, discussions about women in the Torah, suggestions for saying the *Amidah* prayer, concepts of Jewish mysticism.

In my class the other students were much younger than I, the same age as my daughters. Joking about their new Israeli boyfriends, sharing stories of college life, they were at the yeshivah because their American parents required this commitment in exchange for a summer of freedom in Israel. What was I, a middle-aged woman, doing in their company?

At first I considered dropping out of the program, so strong was my discomfort. I had pride in myself, having worked hard to reach a high level in American academia and in my professional life. This seemed to be a step backward. But then I realized that many of these young students knew more than I did. Products of the Jewish education system and alumni of Jewish summer camp, they were comfortable with the material I was just beginning to absorb. Perhaps I could learn from them.

I began to accept my place as an older yeshivah student in this class of giddy college students. In Jewish study, as I was discovering, knowledge levels out other categories. What you know is more important than status, or profession, or how old you are. Learning can begin at any time, and it never ceases.

Indeed, humility seemed to be the most prevalent attitude at this yeshivah. Most of the teachers in the program, orthodox rabbis and a few learned women, modeled this virtue. Open to the new insight and the illuminating detail, listening carefully to the students, encouraging us to argue with each other, they made it clear that there was always more to learn.

Our teachers might have known more than we did, but in the end we were all learners together, or so it appeared. I am reminded of a saying in the Hasidic tradition: "If you know *aleph* [the first letter of the Hebrew alphabet], that is what you teach." These teachers passed on what they knew, but they seemed to understand that parts of the alphabet stretched way beyond their reach, impossible to be absorbed in their lifetimes.

This attitude toward learning never failed to excite me. I remembered the Christianity from my past, where the emphasis seemed to be on the answers rather than the questions. This sets up a certain hierarchy, where the most knowledgeable are looked to as the repositers of truth. But in this yeshivah, I was finding teachers who were also seekers. And I was discovering that Judaism is a religion of questions.

At the yeshivah my classes lasted through the morning and into the early afternoon. Afterward I stuffed my notebook into my bag, and headed toward the center of the city, where I stopped by the falafel stand for lunch.

Sometimes I wandered around the city until dinner, investigating the archeological museums and little shops.

In the evenings Michael and I went to a lecture on the weekly Torah portion, or a cultural event, or a political meeting. Often people would drop by the apartment. More often, in the tradition of Israeli hospitality, we were invited to someone's home for dinner. Most of these invitations came from friends of Michael's from the past, and I, the shy newcomer, listened to the discussion, contributing when I could, but mostly learning about this different culture and the complexities of Israeli politics.

The friendliness of the people I met helped to heal some of the wounds I had received in the orthodox shul in California. They asked me only the most rudimentary questions about myself, accepting me as one more American in a city filled with tourists. I began to relax in their presence.

I never told anyone that summer that I was not yet a Jew. Even the people at the women's yeshivah did not know. In my mind, I was almost converted, so it wasn't much of a falsehood. Besides, no one asked. In truth, I was afraid I'd be rejected if I were honest, and I could not bear it after my experience in the orthodox community.

Passing myself off as a Jew made me heady with anticipation for the time when I actually converted. However, this pretense gave me uncomfortable moments.

One day I was sunbathing at the swimming pool with an American woman who now lived in Jerusalem. "What's your Hebrew name?" she asked.

Thrown off balance by her question, I started to answer that I didn't have one, but she interrupted before I had a chance. "Oh, how stupid of me! Your name must be Hannah, from Nan, right?"

"Right," I replied. In that moment I vowed to myself that when the time came to pick a Hebrew name for my conversion, it would not be Hannah.

During that summer of Jewish immersion, I'd often sit alone in an outdoor cafe, watching people as they passed. I was preoccupied with my appearance, wondering if I stood out as a non-Jew. Even though I wrapped my reddish-brown hair in a silver blue scarf in the Israeli fashion, and wore long, draping skirts, I feared that my background was obvious. I looked for people with fair complexions and blue eyes like mine, and when I saw them speaking Hebrew, as I often did, I was momentarily reassured.

The list of worries continued. There were plenty of Jews who had my coloring, but what about my features? And my behavior, too? I was more contained than many of the Israelis I was meeting and the Jews I knew in America. My first impulse was to hold back rather than to reveal myself. It took time for me to allow the more expressive side to come forward with people I didn't know. I'd nod and smile in a polite way, as I had learned in my Anglo-Saxon Protestant family, letting the other person lead the conversation until I warmed up.

That summer I believed that I revealed my cultural shaping with each gesture I made, or forgot to make. I wanted so much to fit in that I tried to become a different person. Observing those around me, I mimicked their patterns of speech and borrowed their mannerisms, talking faster, moving my hands through the air. This effort was not entirely conscious. Only in retrospect do I see how hard I tried.

Later I would give up this attempt to wipe out the obvious traces of my heritage, but at that time I hoped to succeed. The fact that I hadn't yet converted made me optimistic.

With a lot of effort, I assumed I'd figure it out. Not questioning whether I really wanted to, not accepting how different I really was, not realizing what I was doing to myself, I took on the task, just as I took on the task that summer of studying the Torah and reading *midrashim*.

The question remains: Why would a woman who was relatively secure within herself, and who had clung fiercely throughout her life to her own identity, try to become someone she wasn't? In retrospect it surprises even me. Yet I had my reasons. I was reacting to the attitude many Jews have toward Gentiles. I had overheard enough distrustful, stereotypical comments about people like myself to feel wary. My conversion was the end point of my spiritual journey, one of the most important acts of my life, and I wanted it to go well.

In my talks with other converts I have learned that this remaking of the self is not at all unusual. Converts want to be acceptable, and if it means shaving off some of this or adding some of that, then it seems worth it. The idea of going to all the trouble to convert, only to be rejected, is too painful to contemplate.

However, this attempt to change is a losing proposition. No matter how hard we try, no matter how quick a study we are, we cannot be anything other than who we are: marked ethnically by the family and culture to which we are born.

It would take several years for me to make peace with this. Meanwhile, a few days before Michael and I were scheduled to return to the States, we dropped by the apartment of an older Israeli couple who had befriended us. Sitting in their living room amid their Jewish artifacts and books, I felt the eyes of the man settle on me. "So, what is your background?" he asked.

This was the most direct question about my ethnicity I had received all summer. A few seconds went by in which I was convinced that he suspected I wasn't Jewish. Should I tell him the truth, or should I pretend? In that moment I felt I would lose something of value whatever I said. If I revealed my background, he would not feel so warmly toward me, and if I didn't tell the truth, I'd be caught in a lie. To my relief, his wife came into the room with a tray of shortbread cookies and coffee, and he did not press me further.

The incident gave me an uneasy feeling. But this was only the shadow side of my experience that summer. In my memory those months in Jerusalem remain a time of sweetness and simplicity. They have a dreamy quality, of things unformed, of gazing at the sky, of wandering through the streets, of lingering over books.

When little orthodox boys reach the age of three or four, they are taken on the laps of their fathers or grandfathers and given a stick of candy as they begin to learn Torah. In this way they associate learning with sweetness. I did not receive gifts of candy as I studied that summer, but I made a similar connection between becoming Jewish and sweetness.

When it was time to leave Jerusalem, Michael and I tidied our little apartment and packed our bags. Saying goodbye to the woman next door who fed hamburger to the neighborhood cats, we piled into the *sherut*. As we wound down the mountain road toward the airport, past the pine forests and the war memorials, I held onto these last moments. The summer had been idyllic, and I did not want to let it go.

Back in California, the pleasure of that first trip to Israel quickly faded. Nothing had improved in my absence. When I saw my children, I happily embraced them, but the distance between us had grown. This was evident in their clipped answers to my questions, and in the tentativeness of my own voice.

How could I explain what the summer had been like? The details about traditional Jewish living that I learned in the yeshivah were foreign to them, yet they now shaped my daily life even more. We could only rely on our love and goodwill.

When I telephoned the conservative rabbi, he already had heard that my conversion in Israel did not take place. I never learned the source of his information, but I was not surprised, because by then I realized that news travels fast in the Jewish world. The rabbi was friendly on the phone, but a little distant, or so it seemed. I finally found the courage to ask if he had continued to be harassed by the orthodox congregation. "Yes," he answered. "In the middle of the night. It's gotten worse."

I hung up the telephone, unsure what to do. How could I ask this man to continue with my conversion? He and his family had suffered enough unpleasantness on my account. I would have to find another rabbi, it seemed.

Years later, the conservative rabbi told me that he would have been happy to finish my conversion. "Why didn't you call me back?" he asked. "I'd have gone the full nine yards." And years later, I wondered why I was so unsure of his support, so afraid of being a burden, that I didn't even check with him to see how he felt.

The selection of a rabbi is complicated for most converts. I had gotten along well with the conservative rabbi, exchanging ideas in a spirit of give-and-take. Both of us had been political activists in the sixties, and our concern about *tikkun olam,* healing the world, helped us understand each other. Who would I find to take his place? I wanted someone I could trust with my vulnerability.

And then there was the political question, the matter of what kind of conversion to arrange. In Israel the orthodox establishment controls who is and isn't a Jew. Orthodox conversions in 1985 were the only ones that were recognized as legitimate. If I ever wanted to live in Israel, it was in my interest to be converted by an orthodox rabbi. Although this hadn't been an issue before the summer in Jerusalem, it now was, because I was beginning to dream about the possibility.

Round and round I went. I wanted my conversion to be an experience of spiritual depth. Although I had only a hazy idea of what this would be like, it seemed most possible with a reform, or conservative, or Jewish renewal rabbi. I had heard stories of orthodox conversions that were so perfunctory, so unfeeling, that the new converts felt as if they had been whisked along an assembly line.

And another factor: Even though I had been going to the orthodox shul and had studied at the orthodox women's yeshivah, I thought I would not end up following the orthodox tradition in a strict way. Once I sifted through everything I learned, I would leave behind those parts I couldn't accept. It seemed hypocritical for me to have an orthodox conversion.

As I was considering all this, I returned one Saturday morning to the orthodox shul for Shabbat services. There, in the sparse little room, I slid into a folding chair in the women's section and began *davvening,* praying, along with everyone else. The months in Jerusalem had made me more knowledgeable about this liturgy, and I felt proud of how I could follow along. As often happens, I was moved into a meditative state by the beautiful melodies and the evocative Hebrew words, and soon had a feeling of great joy. It was good to be back.

When the service was over I smiled at the woman next to me. *"Shabbat shalom,"* I said, greeting her in the traditional way. She turned aside without answering.

As the congregation gathered for the blessing over the cup of wine, the *kiddush,* I tried without success to talk with several other people. I wished that someone would acknowledge my return from Israel. I had seen the congregrants greet returnees with great warmth in the past, and I wanted that for myself, but it appeared that I was still the pariah.

On the way to Michael's house afterward, I gave vent to my frustration. "I can't stand it!" I said. "It can't go on like this forever."

He didn't have any answers, but he had some news. After a year without a rabbi, the shul was now hiring one. The search committee had finally made a decision, and the new rabbi would arrive within the month. "Maybe he can help us settle this mess," I said, encouraged.

I waited anxiously for the new rabbi to arrive. If I liked him, I might even ask him to convert me. It seemed like a good idea, despite my hesitations about an orthodox conversion. With his stamp of approval I'd be more acceptable, and it would help to heal my relationship with the congregation.

My first opportunity to observe the new rabbi came on the Shabbat before the holiday of Rosh HaShanah, the Jewish New Year. I wasn't prepared for how young he seemed. A small man with a thin, staccato voice, he had just graduated from seminary. His new wife, who wore a stylish hat in the orthodox fashion, seemed even younger, sitting in the front row, listening to him give his *drash,* his sermon. Later I learned she was still a college student.

Ordinarily I would have felt sympathetic toward this young couple. I could imagine his nervousness on taking over his first congregation; with so many learned congregants, he probably felt intimidated. And I could imagine the rebbetzin's experience, too. I had been married at a young age, at nineteen, to a clergyman, and like her, I had sat in the congregation as my husband led church services. Although my husband was a Protestant minister, not a rabbi, the situation seemed the same. I remembered my feelings of disorientation, suspended as I was between being a student and a minister's wife.

Despite my understanding of the new rabbi's situation, however, I was disappointed that he did not have more stature. But I did not want to judge him too soon. Perhaps he was gifted in mediation.

I let several weeks pass until after Simchas Torah, the last holiday of the High Holy Day season, and then I went to see him. Entering the shul study, now filled with his leather-bound books on the Torah and Jewish law, I immediately came to the point. "Rabbi," I said, "I've been studying intensively for conversion for over a year. I've just come back from Israel, and I'm interested in converting as soon as possible."

I was probably this rabbi's first prospective convert.

"Why would anyone want to be a Jew?" he shrugged. "Forget it."

According to the Jewish tradition, a rabbi is expected to discourage a person three times from converting before agreeing to do it. This protocol comes from the concern about not letting in insincere converts. Since I had already overcome the initial discouragement of the conservative rabbi, I was prepared to present my case.

I reeled off some of my reasons, expressing them in a way that I thought would appeal to an orthodox mind: I wanted to be part of the Jewish people. I found the liturgy and way of life full of meaning. I embraced Jewish values. I buttressed my case by telling him that I was learning first-hand about Shabbat and *kashrut*, the rules and regulations about food. I could have told him more about the spiritual journey that had brought me there, and the details of my previous life, but I sensed that he was not interested.

The rabbi fiddled with his pen until I finished, then looked at me directly for the first time. "I've heard some things about you," he said.

To my embarrassment, my eyes filled with tears. "I'm having a hard time in this congregation," I replied. I went on to relate my side of the story to this man whose background could not have prepared him to understand the complexities and moral ambiguities of my life. "Maybe you can heal the rift," I ended.

By his dour expression, I could see that he didn't think this was a good idea. "You must approach these people in the congregation yourself," he said.

"That's not possible."

"Talk to them," he instructed. "See if you can iron out your differences. Then come back to me."

"That's all you can do?" I asked.

"Yes."

Discouraged, I left the rabbi's office. He seemed entirely unwilling to help me with the congregation or take me on for conversion. Still, his reaction might have been part of that tradition of putting roadblocks in front of the convert. As a newly ordained rabbi, I would expect him to be especially diligent about this.

Later I considered the rabbi's instruction to contact those who were causing me trouble. I wasn't enthusiastic about it, but I had been passive in the face of their hostility for too long. Now it was time for me to act. A letter, polite and to the point, seemed to be the best way.

"There's been a misunderstanding," I decided to write. "Can we get together to talk about it? I will call you soon for your answer."

I sent the letter, and several days went by. One evening, trembling with nervousness, I picked up the telephone and made a call. "Can we talk?" I asked.

There was a silence on the other end of the line. "No," the answer finally came. "There's nothing to say."

Having done what I could, disappointed that my effort hadn't worked but relieved that it had been made, I called the rabbi. "I tried," I said, asking for another appointment.

During the fall of 1985 I went back and forth to this rabbi, discussing the situation in the shul. Two more times he instructed me to make contact with my adversaries, which I did, but it was useless. He could not intervene, he said. Meanwhile, we began to study together, and I read the books he assigned and answered his questions, but I missed the stimulating conversations I had had with the conservative rabbi.

The orthodox rabbi seemed to be taking me on for

conversion, although I couldn't be sure. Whenever I tried to get him to commit to it, he'd answer with a vague, "We'll see."

By this time, my patience was beginning to flag. In my conversations with the rabbi I felt more and more contentious. Although I had sat through the classes in the orthodox women's yeshivah without feeling the need to argue an alternative point of view, and although I had absorbed knowledge from the many orthodox texts I had been reading, I became increasingly irritated by the rabbi's doctrinaire line and began to voice my disagreement with several of the traditional Jewish practices.

"How would you feel, having to sit on the women's side of the *mehitzah?*" I asked, referring to the barrier that separates the men from the women.

"I wouldn't care," he answered. "Women have an honored place in Judaism. What does it matter if they sit separately for a few hours a week?"

I argued the point, saying that the *mehitzah* was symbolic of second-class status, and this was something to be concerned about, but I gave up after a while. Clearly we did not see things the same way.

As the weeks passed, I became more obsessed with the congregation's attitude toward me. I had followed the advice of the rabbi and tried to contact my adversaries, but it had not done any good. If anything, I had become more vulnerable now that my desire for acceptance was known. Saturday after Saturday I forced myself to go to services, but I was so uncomfortable that I could not settle into the prayers. Instead, I'd sneak glances at those around me, wondering how they could be so unhospitable. Who were they anyhow?

I began to scheme about retribution. I imagined sending a letter to each member of the congregation, exposing what was going on, blaming them all.

"Dear Member of the Shul," this letter would begin. "I am the stranger in your midst, the woman to whom you have refused to speak for the last ten months. Why do you treat me this way? I am sorry if I have offended you, but it was not intended."

The letter would continue with a reference to *lashon hara*, the law that instructs Jews to not gossip or talk poorly about anyone. I'd let them know how deeply I had been hurt by their disobedience of this law, and finish by reminding them of the often-repeated commandment in the Torah to treat the stranger kindly.

One rainy weekend I fled alone to a beachside town a few hours away. Michael and I had quarreled, and I was desperate for a respite from the shul. But even though I brought along a new novel and a stash of chocolate, I couldn't escape from my unhappiness. In the cramped cabin, with a single kerosene lantern making shadowy patterns on the wall, I spent Friday night and Saturday, all of Shabbat, lying on my bed, worrying about Michael, ruminating about the orthodox congregation, listening to the rain.

And then on Sunday, I took my legal pad from my briefcase and carefully began to compose the letter that had been running through my mind for weeks. "Dear Member of the Shul," it began. I worked and worked on the language, tearing up drafts, making sure that I was fair but firm in my description of what had happened.

My pleasure in writing was strong. The letter would bring the congregants around. Ashamed of themselves, they would immediately decide to treat me better. But when the letter was as perfect as I could make it, my certainty of this change of attitude faded. In reality, I realized the congregants would respond with outrage to my letter, calling each other on the telephone, condemning me. Who was I to tell them how they should be?

I was aghast at my own desire for vengeance. I had spent the whole weekend fantasizing about shaming these people, but I didn't even know them. What was happening to me? Always concerned about pleasing others, never one to go where I wasn't wanted, I seemed to have undergone a personality change. I had become scrappy and ill-tempered, engaged in an ugly power struggle. Now I wanted to get back at the congregation because I was on the losing end of this struggle.

Worst of all, I had become spiritually disconnected. My anger and resentment left little room for me to experience the holiness of life. Hadn't I spent the last twenty-four hours obsessing about these people, rather than sinking into the sweet spaciousness of Shabbat?

The weather was beginning to clear, the sun darting through the gray clouds. It was time to return to Michael's house, but I wrapped myself in my heavy jacket and headed down the beach, stepping over the debris from the season's first storm.

I wouldn't send the letter, I decided. It would hurt only me. Instead I'd fold it into little squares and hide it in the corner of my bureau drawer at Michael's house, where it would remain as a reminder of how I had lost my way on my spiritual journey.

Ten years later I am still sorting out the experience at the orthodox shul. Recently I described it to my friend Sandy. "Those days were terrible," I told her. "But I have to look at my part. I shouldn't have been so stubborn."

"Don't be hard on yourself," she replied. "The situation was impossible."

This conversation took place on one of our Thursday morning hikes through a redwood glade near my house. It was winter, and the thick tule fog swirled in the trees above. "I still don't understand why you kept going to that shul," she said. "You could have found another."

"Yes, but none with the same spirit," I replied. "In orthodoxy everybody knows the prayers."

Sandy's skeptical expression encouraged me to go on. "Besides, that shul showed me the worst of what I was adopting. It showed me the shadow side of Jewish life. It's like knowing your partner's bad habits before you commit yourself."

"What a way to learn," she said. "I wouldn't have done it."

"You were born Jewish. You didn't have to."

We walked together silently for a while. I was pleased I had come this far in my explanation, but I knew I hadn't reached the deepest level.

I began once again: "There's something else. A lesson I'm just now understanding."

Sandy glanced at me curiously as I continued. "It had to do with my fear of rejection," I said. "All my life this fear had great power over me. I was always trying to please everyone, and couldn't be my fullest self."

"A common experience, especially for women," she interjected.

"Right. But for me to become more real, more creative, more honest, I needed to get over this fear," I said. "I had to get beyond what others thought of me. Going to that shul helped me do it. I put myself in the worst possible situation, got rejected, *and* survived. I learned that I wouldn't be decimated if people hated me. It was liberating."

"Interesting that you would do this psychological work in a Jewish place, at the time you were converting to Judaism," she said.

"The two went together," I replied. "The emerging self and becoming a Jew."

"What we go through to get beyond our childhood experience," Sandy laughed. I felt close to her. Nothing more needed to be said. She already knew enough about me to fill in the context: the complicated and confusing closeness with my father when I was a young child, then his abrupt distance as I grew older. The pain of this had been enough to keep me fearful of rejection for years.

We came to a place in the path where a redwood tree had fallen in the most recent storm. Stepping over its leafy branches, I felt satisfied with this new clarity. "In the end I got a lot from that shul," I said, more to myself than to her.

There are layers of meaning to any act. Some are obvious, others are hidden. The experience at the orthodox shul is an example of how one understanding leads to another. I am wary of facile analyses. This is so whether the subject is contained in time, like my experience at the shul, or stretches over a lifetime, like my conversion to Judaism.

As a convert, as one of the 200,000 strangers in the midst of the American Jewish community, I am the object of great curiosity. Since I am publicly identified as a convert, people sometimes overcome their reticence and ask me about my life.

"Why did you become Jewish?" they usually begin,

just as they might ask why I signed up for a course in Yiddish or joined a choral group. I appreciate their interest and respect their desire to learn about my experience. But I often falter as I answer.

I am not comfortable summarizing my experience. The truth is so deeply embedded in my life that I cannot separate it without distortion. When I open my imagination, colors and shapes and sounds swirl together as part of the vortex through which I passed on my way to conversion. And when I add snippets of memories, moments that go with words like creek and grandmother and darkness, the vortex becomes larger. And when I think of Baptist Sunday school, and when I remember my parents' home, and my mother's illness, and the way we said grace around the dinner table, and the first time I heard about the Holocaust, I understand even more; and it goes on from there, so that everything I've experienced is significant in the same way that a drop of iodine poured into water is diffused throughout.

All my life experience is connected to my conversion. Although this is my truth, a question remains. How, then, do I explain myself to people who are sincerely interested in knowing more about me? If I brush them off, I am not allowing an intimacy that can come through shared stories.

I sometimes tell people I converted after a long spiritual journey. This is an important part of my story: My experiences of spirituality as a child. My disillusionment with Christianity as an adult. The years as an atheist. My awakening to a consciousness of the divine. The move toward Judaism.

But if I rush through this life experience, it sounds trite and predictable, diminished in my own eyes. And if I condense it under the category of spiritual journey, people look at me blankly. The idea of a spiritual journey is so vague that I've not really told them anything.

I can always say that I converted because of my relationship with Michael. Most people assume that this is so, anyhow. An act of love, a renegation of self to please the beloved. Hasn't it been this way throughout history? Woman, the passive and pliant sex, taking on the religion of the lover, the husband.

When I hear this assumption about my past, I have an immediate reaction. "No, that's not what happened," I state loudly. "My conversion is for me." I want to say: Who do you think I am? Don't you know that I take my commitment to Judaism very seriously? Don't you understand that I became a Jew after decades of consideration and preparation, and I did it for myself, as it had to be?

Yet the truth is that I converted partly because of Michael. Although I had been moving in that direction for years, he was the impetus for me actually doing it. He opened his home to me, shared his understanding of Judaism, introduced me to the beauty of Shabbat. His support and guidance during the process made it all the easier. Although I believe I would have converted eventually, the issue of conversion was brought more to the foreground by our relationship and by his desire that I be a Jew.

Through the years I have spoken with many converts. Wherever I go, they seek me out, tell me their stories, talk about their problems. Often I lead workshops for them, in an effort to make clearer our struggle. Several years ago I interviewed two dozen of them in depth in an attempt to better understand my own experience.

I have met many women who at first glance appear to have converted for marriage. Their story seems uncomplicated: they met a Jewish man, fell in love, and converted because he wanted it. But always, as with me, there is more. A hunger for connectedness, a disenchantment with the religion of their birth, a desire for spiritual meaning, an interest in creating a close-knit family within a supportive community, an intellectual fascination. These reasons, and others, existed well before the woman met the man, so that the choice of a Jewish mate was part of the resolution of these issues.

People become Jewish for very complex reasons. If a convert says, on asking, that it was done because of spiritual insight or marriage, this is only the most obvious explanation.

The roots of conversion go back to childhood. For some, there is an identification with a Jewish relative, perhaps a great-grandfather who married a Gentile woman, or an aunt by marriage who was Jewish. These converts often feel that they are claiming their true identity by becoming Jews, correcting a matter that has been too long ignored.

Other converts attribute their first interest in Judaism to someone they knew as a child, a Jewish best friend or the Jewish family down the street where they felt welcomed. But many, like myself, did not have close connections with Jews. Although a few Jewish children lived in my northern California suburban town, they were not my friends. I was fascinated by the thick, long braid of Abigail, whose father was a rabbi, but I saw her only on the school bus. After learning about the Holocaust as a teenager, I wanted to talk with her and the other Jewish students in my high school about that unfathomable event, but I did not have the nerve. The gulf between us was too wide. I was the one creating it: I had been taught by my Christian culture that Jews were different, and that the Jewish religion was honorable but somehow inferior.

My connection to Judaism was hardly existent. But even people like me have a link with their past: a relationship that was instrumental, or an experience of pain, or something that touched us or gave us meaning, so that when we later make the decision to convert, the connection exists between our earliest days and this new identity.

Many converts tell me that they have been aware of the spiritual dimension of life from the time they were very young. They experienced it sitting in a tree, or gazing at the stars, or floating in water. This early awareness in nature, though it had nothing to do with Judaism, shaped their spiritual search and eventually led them to convert.

Such was my experience. As a child, I had a secret place I used to visit every day, a creek that ran close by my family's house. This was where I went to be alone. After school I left my shoes by the side of the road and slid down the narrow, muddy path to this creek. Sometimes the spring rains filled the creek bed with rushing water, but most often there was just a trickle, and little pools formed by rocks.

I was surrounded there by fecundity: Ferns, rotting leaves, undergrowth. Slimy rocks and mud. Everything was a part of everything else, and boundaries did not exist. I explored this creek, moving quietly so as to not disturb the stillness. My body became one with my surroundings, large in the narrow straits and small next to the high creek-bed wall.

Sometimes I stared into the water, merging into its depths. I watched the little tadpoles dart from rock to rock. Happy there, and filled with a sense of peace, I closed my eyes and let myself be part of the sounds around me.

The image of the creek is often with me in Jewish services. When I say the *Sh'ma,* I remember the smell of the clay, the color of the vegetation, the cool of the water. *"Sh'ma Israel, Adonoy Eloheinu, Adonoy Ehad."* In English, "Hear, Israel: Adonoy is our God, Adonoy is One." These words speak of the connectedness of all life that I first came to know at the creek.

When I was a child, I did not have a name for this experience of oneness. "I'm going exploring," I'd tell my mother, rushing out the door to the creek. "Don't get dirty. Be back for dinner," she'd reply, always concerned about tidiness and punctuality. She did not know that I was on my way to an experience of wonder, and that the creek today would be different from the day before and the day after.

In later years I came to recognize that what I felt at the creek was spiritual in nature. The understanding of the union of all life never left me, although at times it grew distant. Then I yearned for it without knowing.

Awakened to spiritual experience in childhood, I did not question its existence. But this in itself was not enough to lead me to Judaism. I could have continued finding spirituality in nature without adopting a religion, as so many people do. I could have been satisfied with walks in the woods, and moonlight hikes, and quiet moments in the fern grove at the state park.

But I always understood that there was another possibility, a deeper integration of spirituality into everyday life. The meditative time at the creek was central in my experience, but it was not the full extent of spiritual experience.

Grandma Alice, my father's mother, taught me that other possibilities exist. A Christian fundamentalist, she believed strongly in the power of religion, and most strongly in the power of the church. Here, too, was a place where one could find spiritual fulfillment.

My passage into Judaism covered the course of two decades, from the time I was in my twenties until my mid-forties. During those years, and in the decade since my conversion, I have felt the presence of this grandmother. She was part of my becoming Jewish, although such an idea seems preposterous, given the differences between Christianity and Judaism.

When I think of Grandma Alice, I picture her in the old house in Covelo, a day's drive north of the San Francisco Bay Area. My parents, my two brothers, and I sometimes visited her and Grandpa Ed in the summertime when I was a child.

For hours at a time, Grandma Alice would bang out hymns on the upright piano in the living room parlor. "On a hill far away, stood the Old Rugged Cross, the emblem of suffering and shame," she'd sing. "I will cherish that Old Rugged, Old Rugged Cross, and exchange it someday for a crown."

Grandma missed many of the piano notes, and her voice was off-key, but her intensity was something to witness. I'd sneak into the room and watch her, an old woman dressed in a baggy half-sized dress and heavy black shoes, hunched over the piano, pounding the keys with her arthritic fingers. The look on her face was pure light. She was in such a state of what she called grace that she seldom noticed me.

Grandma's religious passion was not confined to singing hymns. Most conversations ended up with her preaching, to everyone's consternation. In the evening after dinner, as the family sat around the kitchen table talking about the crops in the valley or a distant cousin who had become a missionary, she'd begin to preach. At first my parents would try to change the subject, but their efforts proved useless against Grandma's determination.

"Christ died for your sins," she'd say, looking directly at me and my older brother. "He's your savior, remember that." Coming from her, it sounded like an indictment.

One by one, everyone slipped away from the table: my Grandpa Ed, who hardly spoke, then my parents and my brothers. I'd be the only one remaining. My grandmother continued preaching about Jesus, shaking her finger at me, instructing me to fear God's judgment and obey the law of loving your neighbor as yourself. I'd grow weary of listening, but I remained fascinated by her enthusiasm.

At the orthodox shul, Grandma Alice would have fit in. With her biblical fervor and her fist raised in the air, she had the same temperament as some of the people there. Grandma needed to pray someplace where she could make noise, sing loudly, shout "Amen!" That shul even looked like the church she belonged to in Covelo: a simple, small building, with blue and white interior and light filling the sanctuary.

But there is something else. Perhaps I loved Grandma Alice more than I realized. I didn't see her often, only when she came to our house or when we made the day's drive to Covelo. And at those times she hardly paid attention to me; she was too busy studying the Bible, or trying to convince everyone to love Jesus.

Yet once I crawled into Grandma's double bed in Covelo, and she wept. It was early morning, before anyone else was awake. I was on my way back from the bathroom. "Are you cold?" she asked as I passed through her room. I nodded, and she made a place for me beside her in the warm bed. Her silver hair, which she always pinned at the top of her head, was tousled from sleep, and she smelled fresh, like laundry soap.

In the half-lit room I began to ask about her mother, my great-grandmother. Shy from this unexpected intimacy, I could not think of anything else to say. I don't remember my grandmother's words, but I can still hear the sound of her voice as it softened into sadness. "I miss her so," she whispered. Tears ran down her face, and she choked back sobs. I watched as she tried to compose herself.

Soon she pointed to a picture of Jesus on the wall, the shepherd cradling a lost sheep, and she spoke about how he comforts people in need. I lost interest, wishing that she would weep again. I had never seen a grown-up reveal so much, and I felt that I was in the presence of something miraculous.

Afterward, it seemed that this moment between us had never existed. She did not pay any more attention to me than before. Yet I felt attached to her, and loved her, and she became even more the object of my interest. Surely someone who allowed such tender feelings must hold important knowledge. The knowledge was not in what she said; it was there in her presence.

I often think of Grandma Alice when I read Jewish texts. She used to study the Bible every day, cramming notes in the margins and on the empty spaces around the printed words. "Trust ye the Lord!!" she scribbled in red pencil on the Bible she gave me when I was eight. "Seek and ye shall find!!!" When she died, she left behind hundreds of Bibles and books, filled with her cramped handwriting and exclamation points.

I can easily imagine my grandmother as one of Chagall's black-suited whirling Hasids. She would have been happy studying Talmud and Hasidut in the yeshivah all day, arguing about the fine points of the law, dancing and singing with the other Hasidim, praying morning, afternoon, and evening, welcoming in the Sabbath with full fervor. For her that would have been a life of ecstacy.

I am writing here about Grandma Alice to reveal how complicated the connections are that bring converts into Judaism. It is like the song *"Chad Gadya,"* sung at Passover: "The ox came and drank the water that quenched the fire that burned the stick that beat the dog. . . ." If I hadn't had the experience at the creek, I might not have paid so much attention to Grandma Alice. And if she hadn't been my grandmother, I might not have been so interested in religion, and so it goes, one thing leading to another, ending up with me as a Jew.

But even this is simplifying my experience too much. The path to Judaism is not straight. In the task of sorting through why I made such a huge change, I look at every relationship, every experience. I've discovered the connection between the creek and Grandma Alice, and my Judaism, but I know this to be just the beginning.

In the fall of 1985, while trying to birth myself as a Jew, another gestation was taking place. Michael and I were beginning to create a magazine.

By this time we had bought a home together, high on a hill looking out over the water, with enough room for Michael's son to live and my children to stay when they visited. Michael's old house was now our office. Every day we went there to work on this new project.

The idea of the magazine came from the discussions we had had for the past year, since we met, about the lack of vision in the American political left, and the apathy and hopelessness among those who consider themselves to be politically progressive. When we asked ourselves what we could do about this, we kept coming back to the power of the written word. Its influence on policy and consciousness had certainly been demonstrated through history.

Many people have the desire to start a magazine, but few actually are able to do it. We were fortunate in that I was not bound by a job. Michael also had free time, as he had just finished a large project at the Institute for Labor and Mental Health. With enough money to get off the ground and the possibility of funding from other sources, we had an opportunity that might never come our way again.

The original plan for the magazine had been to focus on politics and psychology, since both of us were familiar with these subjects. But after Jerusalem, and after so much intensive study about Judaism, this conception didn't seem right. Neither of us had any interest in putting all our time, energy, and money into creating something that left out religion and spirituality.

The magazine would have a Jewish identity, we decided. Its editorial voice would be progressive, and it would cover a wide range of topics, from American politics to cultural issues to subjects of Jewish interest.

When we described this conception of the magazine to friends, they were not very enthusiastic. Who would be interested in such an amalgam? And when we picked the name *Tikkun,* because no other name had the right meaning, their response was uniform. "A Jewish name? What a mistake! It's unfamiliar, and it will just turn people off." But by that time we were beyond listening, because the image of this magazine burned so strongly within us that it didn't matter if anyone else liked it.

I now am struck with how my identity as a separate being became merged with Michael's into a "we" that created this magazine. It was as though we were one organism, moving along without a head or a tail, more like an amoeba, multiplying cells, expanding. In our common mind, decisions were made without knowing who said what first.

But in reality, major differences existed between us. Most obvious were our varied styles. Michael was outspoken and directive, and I was calm and conciliatory. But just as important were the widely divergent experiences we brought to the magazine. Michael had been at the center of the radical political movement in the sixties, and I had been on the fringes, living in the Midwest. And I was not yet a Jew, while he had had a lifelong involvement with Judaism and the Jewish community.

Both perspectives were crucial in creating a magazine that would reach a wide spectrum of people. I understood the issues of unaffiliation better than the issues of affiliation, and Michael, the reverse. Even though I grasped that this difference between us was useful, it was easy for me to forget. From the beginning, I felt unsure of myself, and self-conscious because my political experience had not been greater and my connection to the Jewish world was so tenuous.

Meanwhile, I was relieved to be back at work. In the evenings I continued my Jewish learning, but now my days had a larger purpose. Neither of us knew anything about the business of publishing, so in those early stages of firming up the magazine's conception, we scurried around, trying to figure out what needed to be done.

Our first task was to gather together a national editorial board. It would represent all parts of our projected constituency. Nobody would be left out, from secular Jews to orthodox Jews, from radical leftists to middle-of-the-road intellectuals.

When we made lists of possible names, my lack of familiarity with leaders in the political and Jewish worlds became obvious. "It's yours to do," I told Michael. "This is the time when you can pull in your chips." He laughed, taking this as a challenge to put together a stellar board. Soon we had seventy names.

Many decisions had to be made right off about the size and style of the magazine, promotion, and subscriptions. I'd often call other publishers to ask for advice. "I'm involved in starting a magazine," I'd begin. When asked what kind of magazine, I'd say that it was Jewish. This description felt so peculiar, so unbelievable coming from me, a woman who wasn't born Jewish and who hadn't even yet converted, that I'd quickly add, "But the magazine's also about politics, culture, and society."

The amount of disorientation I felt at that time can hardly be exaggerated. I was starting a Jewish magazine, putting all my resources into it. It seemed to be the right thing for me to do, and I was deeply committed to the project. But when I stopped to think about it or when I described it to others, it sounded absolutely inappropriate.

As long as I was learning about magazine circulation, or studying different magazines in the bookstores to get design ideas, I was on solid ground. These tasks did not require Jewish experience or years of political involvement. But when I explained the magazine to a potential editorial board member, acting more sure of myself than I was, I had a feeling of unreality.

Creative projects do not seem real at first, of course. An act of faith is required, a belief that something of worth will come of all the effort. But my sense of unreality was more than this. Who was I to start this magazine? Acutely aware of the missing parts of my experience, I tried to remind myself that experience wasn't everything, that sometimes the newcomer or the beginner can see things that the more seasoned person cannot.

Still, this unsettledness about my relationship to the magazine made me all the more anxious to complete my conversion to Judaism as soon as possible. Although I understood and respected the idea that it shouldn't be rushed, that it should be savored in each stage, that it had its own mysterious timing, I grew increasingly impatient with the orthodox rabbi. Hadn't I proven my commitment to Judaism by now?

In the midst of this, Michael and I left town one weekend for a retreat in the Santa Cruz mountains led by

Rabbi Zalman Schachter-Shalomi, the founding rabbi of the Jewish renewal movement. This was to be my first real exposure to Jewish renewal, although I had had a taste of it a few weeks earlier at the Yom Kippur service at a local Jewish renewal congregation.

Michael had encouraged me to attend that earlier service, saying he thought I would like it. The Jewish renewal movement is at the progressive end of the religious continuum, with its concern about social justice and the inclusion of marginal Jews into the community. Its services are often innovative, mixing Hebrew with English and traditional prayers with poetry and meditation.

Indeed, the Jewish renewal service had moved me that day. People expressed their emotions in a free way, reaching out their arms during the prayers, weeping as they sang *"Avinu Malkenu."* Both women and men led the prayers, which was a relief to see. When I returned to the orthodox shul for the concluding Yom Kippur service at sundown, I knew I'd return to this Jewish renewal congregation in the future.

With much anticipation, then, I arrived at Rabbi Zalman's Jewish renewal weekend retreat. Although I didn't recognize anyone in the group as we registered, the atmosphere was friendly. Gathering for the opening service on Friday night in the lodge, I looked with appreciation at the excited faces in the circle, and Rabbi Zalman's kind face. Zalman led us in songs and reflection about the week we left behind, bringing us into the holy space of Shabbat. Surely this was a most beautiful flowering of Judaism.

As the weekend progressed, I attended all the sessions, listening as Zalman told stories and taught us about the prayers. Connecting Judaism to aspects of our lives like software programming and psychic phenomena, and referring to other religions with appreciation, he pushed the boundaries of Judaism back so that there was more room for people like me.

I was intrigued by this different way of being Jewish. Still, I felt tense that weekend, and hardly joined in the conversation between sessions. Worried about my conversion, concerned about my relationship to my children, I had a lot on my mind.

But there was something else that kept me separate. I felt like an outsider. Among these people who were similar to me in so many ways, my differentness seemed even more apparent, at least to me. It was there in the way I held back from expressing myself, and in the things I would have said, had I dared.

At the orthodox shul I never expected to feel that I was with people of my own kind. Even if there hadn't been the problem with the congregation, the political and lifestyle differences between us were so great that if I had been born Jewish, I still wouldn't have fit in. But in this group at the retreat, I should have felt comfortable. It was a disappointment that I didn't.

Part of the difficulty existed because I was hiding the fact that I was not yet a Jew. I hadn't planned to do this. I simply never got around to revealing the truth of my identity. This was a repeat of the past summer's experience. No one asked, and it would have seemed strange to blurt it out after the retreat had been under way for a while.

However, the Santa Cruz mountains were closer to my home than Jerusalem. In my community people knew about my non-Jewish background because of the gossip at the orthodox shul. If some of these people at the retreat were to talk to those in my community, I'd be shown up as a deceiver. It all seemed so complicated. I couldn't figure out what to do, so I kept quiet about my past, carefully monitoring everything I said. This effort made me self-conscious and awkward, and it drained my energy. No wonder I hardly connected with anyone that weekend.

The hardest moments came when people discussed their childhood experiences or family history, as they often seemed to do. Then I felt the most vulnerable, because whatever I said might reveal too much. At lunch on Saturday the people at my table were talking about their families and when they arrived in the United States. "And you? What about yours?" the woman next to me asked.

For a moment I froze. "They came from England, but they've been here a while," I answered. I hoped that this response would not give me away. Although I hadn't lied, I also hadn't revealed the full truth: my family has been in America since the eighteenth century, and none of my ancestors were Jewish.

As the weekend retreat came to a close, everyone gathered on the lodge porch for Zalman's last session. Shadows were already forming, and soon it would be time to pack up the car and go home. Zalman was telling a funny story about a Hasidic rabbi, but I hardly listened. An hour before, I had decided to approach him with my problems, and I was nervously rehearsing my speech.

"Zalman, can I speak to you," I said, grabbing his arm when he had finished and the group cleared around him.

Without asking what was on my mind, he steered me over to a dark corner of the porch and pulled two chairs together so that we could talk privately. "*Nu?*" he said. "So?"

"I'm converting to Judaism, and I'm having a hard time," I told him. There, it was out.

"I see." He paused. "I noticed something different about you this weekend. Although you know the songs and the prayers, I could tell you aren't a Jew." He peered at me through the darkness, and I flinched, disappointed that I hadn't passed after all.

"Perhaps you have the soul of one who was killed during the Holocaust, and you are returning now to finish what was unfinished," he said. Another long pause. "Yes, I think that's how it was. When were you born?"

"Nineteen-forty," I answered.

The logistics seemed improbable, but he sighed, "Ah, it still might have been. You might have been one of the earliest."

This was the first I had heard about converts being returning souls. I hardly knew what to make of it, although I felt pleased that he included me in this category. "I'm converting with an orthodox rabbi I don't like," I confided.

He paused for several more moments, filling the shadowy space with his presence. "Here's what you should do," he said. "When the time comes for the conversion, stay up the whole night before. Make sure you are alone. Go deep within yourself. Take a little something to help you do this, if you wish, and understand what this conversion means to you."

I imagined climbing to the top of the mountain behind our house and spending the night there, under the stars. In the morning I'd come down just in time to go to the *mikveh* for my conversion with the orthodox rabbi. After such an experience, perhaps I would be so full of understanding that my feelings about the conversion wouldn't matter. "That's a good idea," I said, wondering if it would work.

The darkness and Zalman's soft intonation had put

me into a relaxed state by this time, and I waited to hear what else he would say. "Don't throw away the things you've learned in your past life," he told me. "If something has had meaning for you, hold onto it. Becoming Jewish is like coming home. You can bring everything from your past travels."

The image of homecoming appealed to me. It seemed to express the essence of my conversion. Becoming Jewish was returning to a familiar place, rather than journeying to a foreign land. Although I hadn't been raised Jewish, I felt at home in Judaism. I often thought that I must have been put into the wrong slot when I was born.

I welcomed the idea of bringing along everything with me from my past life. In traditional Judaism converts are considered born anew at the time of conversion, and encouraged to sever their emotional ties with the past. Despite my effort at this retreat to conceal my non-Jewish background, I chafed with this instruction. Why cut myself off emotionally from the valuable lessons learned in my lifetime, the important experiences I had had? I did not wish to diminish my connection to those I loved who were not Jewish.

As Zalman and I sat quietly together for a few more minutes, I was flooded with images of homecoming. Like a kaleidoscope, the shapes and colors changed into different patterns with each twist of my imagination. Finally Zalman cleared his throat and rose from his chair, the conversation over. As he left, he clasped my shoulder, saying, "Just remember who you are."

The words reverberated in my mind after he left. They sounded wise. Perhaps they would guide me through the complexities of conversion in the next few months. But following his advice wasn't as simple as it sounded. Who was I, anyhow?

After I came back into the lodge, Michael asked how my talk with Zalman had gone. "I'm not sure," I said, still dazed. "I think it was wonderful."

I went on to tell him what Zalman had said about me being a Holocaust soul. "Maybe," he replied. Savoring the moment, I just smiled.

In the days that followed, I thought a lot about the talk with Zalman. Clearly it was a turning point, although I did not know what lay ahead. It wasn't so much what he had said, but that he had taken me seriously, honoring my desire to convert. Even more, he had given me the gift of his imagination and intuition. As a result, I felt less apologetic about myself, and more determined than ever to make my conversion a proud and joyous experience.

As I reviewed my conversation with him, I kept returning to his final advice of remembering who I was. Perhaps this would be the bridge connecting the old world with the new.

I began to think about my past and the meaning of religion for me. Since my decision to convert, I had pushed the Christian part of my background aside. It was too confusing to remember that I once felt love for this religion, too. Perhaps it was time to begin to integrate this, in the spirit of not throwing anything out.

In the midst of those frenetic days of starting the magazine, I'd often go back over my life, remembering what it was like to be a Christian. I'd picture myself as a young child, being dropped off with my older brother at the nearby Baptist church on Sunday mornings. My father would drive us there while my mother slept in late, and he'd give me a few pennies or a nickel to put in the silver offering plate. We were living at the time in a navy-base town across the bay from San Francisco. My father was in the drugstore business, with two stores already in existence and many more planned, and my mother worked at home, caring for the children.

I did not question being sent to Sunday school. After all, my family was Christian, even though my parents did not go to church at that time. The fact that we had a Christian education seems strange to me now, given my parents' secular bent, but Grandma Alice's Christian influence in the family was strong. It was bad enough in her opinion that her son, my father, owned drugstores where liquor, the heathen substance, was sold; she refused to step inside them. But it would have been unthinkable for her grandchildren to grow up without a Christian education.

When my father dropped us off at Baptist Sunday school, I'd go down the steps to the cavernous old church basement and sit in a circle with the other children. There we'd sing "Jesus Loves the Little Children," my favorite song, or "Jesus Wants Me for a Sunbeam." On the wall was a picture of Jesus gazing up at the mountains, his tapered hands folded over his chest. With his flowing gown and his sweet expression, he looked like a woman. Next to this picture was a map of the Holy Land, where we were told that Jesus lived. "Children, this is the promised land," the teacher said.

During the week my family went through the motions of Christian observance. At bedtime my father bathed and dried me, told stories and sang songs. My most nurturing parent, he then lay beside me, reminding me to say my prayers. Folding my hands, like I had seen Grandma Alice do, I'd recite: "Now I lay me down to sleep. I pray the Lord my soul to keep. If I should die before I wake, I pray the Lord my soul to take." I rattled this prayer off like a nursery rhyme, but it left me with a dark, scary feeling, and I'd ask my father to sing another song.

Every evening, when my father came home from work, my family ate dinner together. As my two brothers and I gathered around the table, my mother reminded us to say grace. Bowing my head like I'd been taught, I closed my eyes and chanted: "Thanks to our Father, we will sing. For He gives us everything. Amen." I liked this simple prayer, although in my mind the Father in the prayer was mixed up with my real father, who provided us with money to buy our food.

I don't know where this grace came from. Unlike the *Birkat HaMazon* in Judaism, there is no traditional Christian prayer after meals, so my parents must have heard it somewhere and decided to adopt it in an attempt to reassure Grandma Alice that they were not raising heathen children.

As a young child, being Christian meant going to Sunday school and saying these daily prayers, as well as behaving in a certain way. We were supposed to be kind and loving like Jesus, Grandma Alice told me. I was not interested in Jesus, because he seemed too good, but God was something to reckon with, a super-father who could protect me if I was deserving, or swoop out of the sky and punish me if I was bad.

I also learned about Christian culture. One of the major lessons, coming from my father, seemed to be that white-skinned Christians were the best people in the world. All other people were inferior. Even though my father rejected Grandma Alice's religiosity, he agreed with her on this point.

When I was eight, my family moved to a suburban town further away from San Francisco. This town was in the midst of post–World War II growth, but it still had a country feeling, with hills to roam and oak trees to climb. There my younger sister was born.

My strongest memory from these years is of the creek, where I'd go almost every day. But the community church, a liberal Protestant church in the center of town, became more important to me as I grew older. In the summers my brothers and I were sent there for Bible school. On those sweltering hot days the teacher would talk for an hour about famous people in the Bible, and then we'd get down to the major activity, making wastebaskets out of ice-cream cartons.

During the school year I joined the junior choir. Wearing the white robes that were supposed to make us look like angels, we sang at special church services. *"Panis Angelicus"* became my favorite song, and I practiced it with great feeling when I went down to the creek. There the sound bounced off the creek-bed walls, and the under-growth absorbed the tones.

We were taught in this church to behave in a Christian way, restrained, nice, kind. "That's not being a good Christian," the Sunday school teacher scolded, if we said something mean. This church was higher class and more genteel than the Baptist church of my earlier childhood. With my father's success in the drugstore business, my family was quickly moving up the socioeconomic ladder.

When I reached the eighth grade, I was old enough to join this church. "But I don't believe in Christ," I remember telling the pastor, a white-haired man who liked to tell jokes. Even then, I didn't accept the church's teachings about Jesus; Grandma Alice's early attempts at indoctrination had made me dubious. I thought of Jesus as a kindly man, but not as "Christ, the Son of God, the One Who

Rose from the Dead, My Redeemer, My Lord and Savior."
I complained to the pastor about this, but he reassured me
that I would understand more when I grew older. Feeling
uncertain but proud, I was marshaled through the ceremony of membership.

Around that time my mother became ill with hepati-
tis. A woman who liked peace and quiet, she withdrew to
her bedroom and stayed there for many years thereafter,
struggling to regain her health. For me this was a great
loss. We had become close just before she became ill, and I
felt bereft. Who would help me grow into womanhood in
these next years?

I felt very much alone. My father, who had nourished
me so much when I was small, was now distant. My
younger brother and sister needed him more, and his work
and other interests increasingly occupied his time. The
closeness with him in my early years left me with a longing
for him, and I was angry at his withdrawal. I both
mourned his absence and spurned him when he tried to approach me. As a teenager, our contact was reduced to
silent meals and occasionally arguments.

With my mother ill and in her bedroom, and my father gone much of the time, the atmosphere in our home
grew sad and disconnected. I had no choice but to grow up
quickly, caring for my brothers and sister as best I could,
keeping a watchful eye on my mother.

In my teens I became involved in the church youth
group. Soon I was a leader, giving sermons about faith and
hope, writing prayers, organizing meetings, traveling
around the state to speak at rallies. I was inflamed by the
message I was spreading, like Grandma Alice. However, I
was not trying to make people into Christians, but to remind them to work for the betterment of humanity. In my

sermons I quoted from the Old Testament prophets about seeking justice. I later discovered that my words reflected one of the major tenets of Judaism, *tikkun olam,* the responsibility to heal and repair the broken world.

Like my Jewish friends who trooped off to Camp Ramah each summer, I went to church camp. The atmosphere there was permissive, which gave me the opportunity to be with my boyfriend. My passion for religion became mixed with my sexual awakening, so that I didn't know where one ended and the other began. At the evening campfire my boyfriend and I would find a place on the outskirts of the circle, in the dark, touching each other in forbidden places while the others sang "Steal Away to Jesus" and "Glory, Glory, Hallelujah!"

What did this church have to do with my becoming Jewish? Since I loved it so much as a teenager, it hardly makes sense that I would leave it. But even then, when I was most involved in the church, I had doubts about Christianity. I did not believe in the divinity of Christ, and I was beginning to acknowledge that my father's and Grandma Alice's attitude toward non-Christians was connected to racism.

Still, this church provided a safe haven for me at a time when my own family was falling apart. Just as I had gone to the creek for sustenance as a younger child, I now found it in the church. Without the emotional support of my friends there, and some of the youth advisors and ministers, these years would have been very difficult. "Rocka my soul in the bosom of Abraham," we sang at church camp. It seemed that the church was holding me in a warm place, healing my pain.

Many converts to Judaism are like myself: active in the Christian church at a young age. Recently I read an article by a rabbi who insists that those of us who had this experience are the most devoted converts. The reasoning goes that we make good Jews because we've learned to care deeply about our religious faith. Such a statement seems simplistic, because I have known too many committed converts who had nothing to do with organized religion before conversion. Still, the link in my mind between religion and community was established by the time I was a teenager, and it stayed with me, even after I left the church.

When I graduated from high school, I went off to college in southern California. That first fall was difficult, as I was not prepared for the competition of so many bright students. Returning to my family for the winter holiday break, an event took place that changed the course of my life. I was invited to a New Year's Eve reunion of my old church camp friends, and there I met the man who would soon become my husband.

At the age of nineteen I married the Protestant campus minister at the University of California in Berkeley. He was nine years older than I, articulate, and adept in the social world. Although I had hardly attended church since high school, and already had many misgivings about Christianity, I took on this marriage with determination. I would be a minister's wife, and in that way be connected to the warmth of the church, which I had missed.

Berkeley, where we lived as newlyweds in 1960, was seething with possibilities. Campus politics were heating up, and people talked about radical action. The Free Speech movement was an idea that was finding its form. As a student in the university, where I had transferred after my engagement, I became inflamed by the dreams of those times. Hadn't I always preached about justice?

Yet I was now a minister's wife. I felt the pressure within to be gracious and composed, a good Christian. Although the people at my husband's church did not ask much of me since I was so young, it was clear that my experimental days were over, cut short by a premature vow of diligence and responsibility.

The tension within me grew. My earlier questions about Christianity became foremost in my mind. At dinners with other ministerial couples, and through the tales my husband brought home, I began to witness the inner workings of the church. I was shocked by the hypocrisy that existed: public proclamations against racism were made from the pulpit, but racist actions existed in too many congregations.

It seemed to me that the church was part of the problem of injustice, rather than an answer to it. I began to read more about the persecution of the Jews, and to learn about the history of Christian oppression. Despite my positive experience in the church when I was younger, I increasingly felt that I did not want to be associated with this religion.

I had never accepted the notion of Jesus as Christ, but now I began to question the existence of God. This father-in-the-sky seemed less and less real to me. I remembered the creek, and my experience there, but the Christian God that was expressed in church life did not seem to have anything to do with that deep spirituality. I was an agnostic, or even an atheist, I decided.

When I read Marx's description of religion as "the opiate of the masses" in one of my sociology classes, I felt less alone. My disdain for organized religion became locked into place, where it would remain for many years. Had I stayed in Berkeley much longer, I no doubt would have become involved in the tumultuous political movement of those times. But instead, after I finished my junior-year exams, my husband and I packed up our wedding presents, got on the train, and moved east.

To my relief my husband put his ministerial robes into the closet and settled into graduate work. The traces of Christian observance soon slipped from our life, and in the following years, when I gave birth to three children, I did not think of giving them a Christian education.

This, then, was the end of my relationship with Christianity. A tale of great love and appreciation, but eventual disillusionment and rejection. Now I was choosing Judaism, another religion. Would this commitment end the same way? Such an idea was frightening to contemplate, but in those weeks after talking with Rabbi Zalman, I forced myself to consider it.

I was becoming Jewish as an adult, I reassured myself. Surely this was different from having Christianity thrust on me as a child, or embracing it from emotional need as a teenager. The years of secular living had cleared my vision so that I could see Judaism in a more realistic light, and the path that led me to Judaism had taken enough time for me to understand what I was doing. Any lingering idealization of the Jewish people was being wiped away by my experience at the orthodox shul. No, I decided. There was no comparison in my relationships with Christianity and Judaism. Although I was the same person, my relationship with Christianity had been at the beginning of my religious quest, and I was now at the end.

With this settled in my mind, I went once again to the orthodox rabbi. "Are you willing to convert me now?" I asked.

"How is it going with the congregation?" he replied.

"The same," I told him. "Very few people will speak to me."

The rabbi flipped through the pages of a book on his desk. "I can't convert you until you straighten things out."

I felt my anger begin to rise. "You know it's not all my responsibility."

"Volunteer. Help out. Get involved in the congregation's life by doing *mitzvot*, acts of kindness," he said, closing the book. "After people see that you are sincere, they'll begin to accept you."

"And how long will that take?" I asked bitterly. He didn't answer.

That's it, I decided afterward. Forget the orthodox conversion, at least for the time being. Although I was willing to do almost anything to become a Jew, I would not spend months, years, setting up chairs before events, washing dishes afterward, being kind to people who wouldn't even say hello, waiting for their hearts to soften. The conversation with Rabbi Zalman had given me strength.

Once again, and this time with a feeling of relief, I began to consider what my next step would be. Recently I had been hearing about Rabbi Burt, a man who had a conservative ordination but who now was rabbi of a local Jewish renewal congregation. A social change activist, he had organized his congregation to do outreach into the community, based on the Jewish commitment to *tikkun olam*. He sounded like a good person, someone who might help me have a meaningful conversion, now that I was giving up on the orthodox rabbi.

Rabbi Burt managed to squeeze me into his schedule soon after I called. On the day of our first appointment, I went to his house in the warehouse district of town, and was greeted by three of the hugest dogs I had ever seen. "Quiet!" Burt ordered without success, trying to keep them from jumping on me as he led me through the door and into his tiny study.

A gentle man with a melodious voice, he asked what I wanted. As I explained my situation to him, I felt increasingly comfortable. Here was someone who treated me as an equal, rather than as a supplicant. "I usually require one to two years of study for a conversion," he explained. "People read all the books on my reading list. But since you've had so much experience, we can do it faster."

He listened as I told him what had happened at the orthodox shul. He would do what he could to straighten it out, although he made no promises. "Thanks," I said, grateful for his support. Before I left, we agreed that I'd read a few books he recommended, and we'd meet several more times. Then, he promised, he would arrange for the conversion.

As I ran up the steps to the *Tikkun* office, I felt buoyant. "I'm doing it!" I shouted to Michael as I came through the door. "It's finally going to happen."

Each convert's passage into Judaism is unique. Although mine was not easy, I've heard of some that are more difficult. Many would-be converts never make it to the first step of finding a rabbi, because they are too intimidated by the process. Others get stuck in the beginning stages.

One woman I know took five years to get started. She'd make an appointment with a rabbi, but when he (at that time there were no women rabbis) turned her down three times in the customary way, she felt rejected and didn't return. Only after years of discouragement did she understand that she needed to overcome her timidity and push her way in.

Perhaps this woman was ambivalent about becoming Jewish. I do not know. But the experience of being discouraged by a rabbi is daunting for even the hardiest of souls. Imagine being given the feeling that you're not wanted, or that you're not acceptable—all of this coming at you when you are burning with the desire to become a Jew.

An argument can be made that the process of discouragement is necessary. Like army boot camp, it weeds out those who don't have the commitment or the emotional stamina to handle becoming Jewish. Converting, after all, is much more than embracing Judaism. It requires becoming part of a people that even God called stiff-necked. But there is a fine line between being careful that potential converts are committed and discouraging sincere people so much that they lose heart and walk away.

Converts to Christianity do not go through such a complicated process. They need only to make a statement of Christian belief, and sometimes to be baptized, to be considered Christian.

In Judaism rabbis have all the power. Converts must rely on their goodwill. There is no central organizing board in the United States, no place where a complaint can be taken. In Israel the lack of appeal also exists, even though conversion is under the auspices of the central Rabbinic Court.

This arrangement puts converts in a vulnerable position. When the relationship between convert and rabbi doesn't work, it can cause great pain. But when it does, as it did for me with the conservative rabbi before I went to Israel, and later with Rabbi Burt, it becomes an exciting collaboration. Taking on a teacher is highly honored in Judaism, different from Christian culture where the teacher–student relationship is less emphasized. By being allowed to form this relationship with a rabbi, converts are brought into the community. "My rabbi, my teacher," we can claim, even before becoming Jewish.

After finding a rabbi, the next step for most converts is connecting to a community. This is easiest for those who have a partner or friends active in a congregation, since they can slip in with protection. As with me, however, it doesn't necessarily guarantee acceptance.

Sometimes prospective converts become involved in congregations without revealing their Gentile backgrounds. I know a man who did this. Having studied Judaism in college, he started attending services at the local conservative congregation. Everybody assumed he was

Jewish because he was fluent in Hebrew and seemed to know the liturgy.

Now an active member of his congregation, this man desperately wants to convert. But if he does it in his synagogue, people will discover that he has been tricking them, and their trust in him will be diminished. He is thinking of moving to another city, which he doesn't relish, in order to convert, so that he can come back as a Jew to the community he loves.

Many paths lead to becoming Jewish. Each person finds the way in differently, according to temperament and circumstance. The boundary around the Jewish people is permeable, or at least that is what we are told. But few of us enter without going through permutations of the spirit.

In the days after beginning the conversion process, converts are delicate, like moths in chrysalis. Sensing that the change ahead will be greater than anything we've known, we are both excited and apprehensive. In this way we make our first steps into the Jewish community, unsure of ourselves, constantly watching those around to learn how to act.

Delores, a woman I've met, is in the chrysalis stage. Moving recently to Israel so that she can convert, planning to stay for the rest of her life, she is filled with the light I remember in Grandma Alice's face and the light I must have had in my own ten years ago.

This woman knows a lot about prayer, as she was a lay minister in her African-American church before she decided to become Jewish. At any gathering she is likely to begin praying in the most beautiful, heartfelt way. "Dear God," she says, "Thank you for *baruch*-ing us with your love, and *El*-ing us with your mercy." Those around her look surprised at her use of these Hebrew words, but she is so sincere that they can't help but be moved by this woman who is deeply responsive to the holiness of life.

Now beginning the process of conversion, she must overcome enormous obstacles. In Israel converts return again and again to the Rabbinic Court until they are deemed ready. I've heard stories of discrimination against converts who, like Dolores, are visibly different from most Jews. This includes those who are black, or Asian, or Nordic. Even if these people are deeply committed to Judaism and have taken all the right courses, their conversions sometimes are withheld for years.

One recent day, when Dolores was discouraged by yet another snafu in getting possession of the apartment that she had rented in Jerusalem, she called me. "I've been singing spirituals all day," she said. "That's the only way I keep going." Over the telephone she began to sing about the Lord making us happy when we are sad, and I heard the tears in her voice.

Strung between two worlds, no longer who she once was, but not yet what she will become, she sought solace this time in the spirituals she knew as a child. I've also known her to find it in the Hebrew psalms she loves to recite. This woman, still an innocent, will learn a lot in future years, but I hope that she is spared disillusionment.

Her teacher and friend, Joseph, an ultraorthodox man, is her solace, her lifeline to a Judaism she knows exists. All the rest—the difficulties with the Rabbinic Court, the strangeness of living among Jews—dissipates in his presence. She is fortunate that he is watching over her. He has introduced her to a rabbi who will help her learn what she needs. She is on her way.

*   *   *

In the crucial time before conversion, when everything is so unsure, the teachers and rabbis of converts take on great importance. We look to them for signs of approval and acceptance, but too often we don't find it. Instead we sense ambivalence in the very people who are helping us become Jews.

The reasons for this are complex. Rabbis who work with converts are under pressure to be discerning. They have the responsibility of deciding who gets in and who doesn't, a serious matter for a people who has been so deeply traumatized by outsiders. These rabbis' critical faculties must be operating to make sure that they are not being deceived or missing an important point of information.

This requires a certain vigilance. Converts, after all, are the *goyim*. Even if we appear to be acceptable, we must be watched, because, as one recently published orthodox guide warns, "Much damage has been done to the Jewish people by insincere converts." The author does not elucidate, and I have never found any evidence that supports this statement. Instead, I take this author's admonition as an example of the fear of converts that exists within the Jewish community.

This fear is also evident in the orthodox practice of being careful not to teach the convert too much. "Instruct [him] about a few of the *mitzvot,* but do not teach him Torah," one of the recent orthodox books about conversion says. The dividing line between Jew and non-Jew must be kept, because it is dangerous to impart precious secrets to these questionable people. If they decide not to convert at the last minute, then nothing will have been lost.

Reform and conservative rabbis are less guarded about sharing knowledge. Typically their converts attend classes and read voluminously, so that they end up knowing more than most people who are born Jewish. This process can take a few months for the already educated to several years for the novitiate. Still, there is the watchful eye, the discerning question, the edginess under the surface.

The fear of accepting undesirable converts shows itself most strongly when it comes to marriage. Many people who want to convert plan on marrying a Jew, or are already married to one. The suspicion, then, is that they are going through the motions of conversion to catch a husband or wife, or to placate a Jewish partner.

This suspicion of insincerity filters down onto gay and lesbian converts who have Jewish partners. They are already censured in many parts of the Jewish community for their sexual orientation, and their partnership with a Jew only increases the distrust.

Not surprisingly, the orthodox community is the most concerned about converts in love relationships with Jews. In Israel any hint of this before conversion is grounds for dismissal by the Rabbinic Court. As a result, converts in these relationships must cover their tracks with lies. Those who are already married to Jews face special difficulty. I know of a married woman who was forced to live away from her husband and young child for almost a year in order to convert, until finally a sympathetic rabbi intervened.

Orthodox conversion in the United States is more lenient, but prospective converts in relationships are often looked upon unkindly. I've heard tales about engagements that had to be broken and lovers who were not allowed to see each other before conversion was complete. Many converts are willing to do this because their conversions are so important to them, but others are offended by the suspicion cast upon their motives.

A more tolerant attitude toward converts in relationships exists in the other branches of Judaism. But it often comes from the interest in keeping the married couple Jewish, not the desire to have more converts. Intermarriage is considered undesirable by most Jews. If such a union must take place, there is at least a chance that the children will be raised as Jews if the non-Jewish partner converts.

In recent years a startling fact has begun to surface in the Jewish press. Converts frequently bring their Jewish partners along with them into Judaism. Because they have chosen this tradition as adults, they make it central in their lives and become leaders in their communities. Their Jewish husbands or wives, who never paid attention to Judaism before, now find themselves going to more classes or services than they ever imagined.

The joke is on the man who wants his *shiksa* lover, a symbol of his freedom, to convert for his parents' sake, but not to change. Or the Jewish woman whose nonreligious husband has converted and now insists on observing Shabbat, while she'd rather not. Not surprisingly, difficulties arise between partners. But over time many Jews find that their lives have been enormously enriched, led, as they were, by their convert partner into a deeper relationship to their own tradition.

I am pleased when I hear reports about this happening, because it points to the contributions converts make. If these stories were more widely known, we would be more highly valued. It would help to remove the onus from conversion.

Converts almost always take the commitment of conversion very seriously. I haven't met one yet who doesn't go far beyond the rabbinic category of sincerity, even if a relationship with a Jew exists. To convert solely for the sake of a mate or partner is hardly imaginable. Who would go through the trouble?

As gatekeepers of the Jewish people, rabbis have an important task. But this is not the extent of their role with converts. They are also given the responsibility of caring for them. Sincere converts, the tradition says, are to be encouraged and supported with full vigor. Once accepted for conversion, they are worthy of great effort on the part of the rabbi.

Throughout history there are stories of sages who traveled long distances out of their way to help prospective converts. When I read about them, and when I meet rabbis in the present who are especially helpful to converts, my anger about the often painful process of conversion softens. There are two sides to our reception: suspicion, and exceptional concern and support.

Rabbi Wolfe Kelman, a high official in the conservative movement before his death, embodied the greatest love for converts. I first heard about this from his daughter Naomi, who told me that he believed that converts and women are the hope of Judaism. When I met him, he embraced me, saying the same thing. This one man's belief in my potential helped me feel valued in the community, and gave me courage when I was experiencing so much negativity as a convert.

I also think of Caroline, a woman in New York who soon will convert. She has a standing invitation every Shabbat to her rabbi's house, so that she can sit at the table and eat with Jews on this most high day of the week. The rabbi is concerned that she feel included in the community at a time when she is especially vulnerable.

And I think of a rabbi I know who counseled with a

dying young Gentile man. The dream of this man's life had been to go through conversion, but his illness cut short the process. In the hospital, as he was near death, the rabbi lovingly made him a Jew. It was a simple ceremony, without the examination by the Beit Din, the court of three judges, or a ritual circumcision, or the immersion in the *mikveh,* the ritual pool of water. Most Jews would not consider this conversion *halakhic,* proper according to Jewish law. But what does it matter?

In recent years I have discovered within Jewish mysticism a framework of understanding that supports this kindness to converts. It is attributed to the Vilna Gaon, an eighteenth-century rabbi who taught that the light of creation split when it came down into the world of time and space. One shaft went to the Torah, and the other infused all the wisdoms of the world. Converts bring light from other wisdoms back to Judaism. As the light merges, Torah is revealed in a way that is not possible from the original light itself. A holograph is formed, a dimensionality that cannot exist without light going out and then returning.

Converts, in this view, make a contribution because of their experience in other worlds. We are carriers of light, not supplicants to be suffered. All the effort to teach us, and answer our questions, and sensitize us to Jewish culture and history, is one of the most important tasks of the rabbi or teacher. It is holy work.

In 1986, when I finally converted, I did not know about this. I only understood that some rabbis were hostile, while others seemed to be generous in spirit. To my great relief I had ended up with Rabbi Burt, who was one of the latter.

Three months after our first meeting, Rabbi Burt called me with the announcement that my conversion would soon take place. "I've reserved the *mikveh* on March 12 for you," he said.

I had known that he would speed my conversion along, but I could hardly believe this news. He explained the process to me. "We'll do the conversion at the orthodox synagogue, where the *mikveh* is. Even though I'm not orthodox, and you won't be getting an orthodox conversion, we need to use their *mikveh*."

"Right," I answered, scribbling down his directions to this synagogue, which I hadn't visited before.

"And I've arranged for a woman to be on your Beit Din, the court that will examine you. It wouldn't be appropriate to have you convert with three male judges, not at this time in history." He went on to describe the credentials of this woman, who was a teacher in the community.

"Thanks," I said, greatly appreciating this gesture toward feminism. In all my imaginings of my conversion, I hadn't even thought to insist on including a woman on the Beit Din.

The night before my conversion I remembered Rabbi Zalman's advice to spend time in solitude. I had an evening meeting scheduled, but afterward I went outside on the deck behind our house. Through the redwood trees I saw the night sky, so vast, the stars so far away. I wanted to have an experience of heightened consciousness in these last hours as a Gentile, but it was late and I was tired. Was I still committed to conversion, I asked myself. Yes, of course, I answered. And did I have any regrets? No. With that, I gratefully went inside.

The next morning I awakened early. So much of importance had led up to this day that the details of the experience should be engraved in my mind. But I only faintly recall a brilliant spring morning, chilly enough that I put on my favorite brown wool jacket, the one I wore to my orals for my doctorate a few years before.

As Michael and I drove to the synagogue, I was quiet, wondering what was ahead. Would I be able to answer all the questions at the Beit Din? My anxiety about this merged with my excitement about the day. Trying to calm myself, I looked out the window at the wild plum trees blossoming along the side of the road and the rolling hills in the distance, covered with fresh green grass.

Michael dropped me off in front of the orthodox synagogue where the *mikveh* was. "Just think, by the time I see you again, you'll be a Jew," he said.

"Yes," I answered, amazed that it would be so easy after all the struggle.

The synagogue seemed deserted, and I wandered through the unfamiliar corridors looking for Rabbi Burt. Should I call his name? Finally I went through a half-opened door, and found him in a little room with the other members of my Beit Din, a man and woman who I had not met before.

After introductions and a few moments of small talk, Burt had us sit in a circle. "Let us begin," he said in a formal way.

As though I were back in front of my orals committee, I answered the questions that were directed at me. Some of them were difficult, but I quickly understood that my interrogators were not concerned that I know everything. The point was to see if I could converse in these areas.

Only a few questions remain now in my memory:

"What is the importance of *mitzvot,* and how many are there?"

"Who were the seven women in Moses's life?"

"Who was Maimonides, and what was his thinking?"

"How do you interpret the happening at Mt. Sinai?"

I do not recall how long the questioning went on, although it lasted at least an hour. Somewhere in the middle, I began to relax enough to let myself feel the preciousness of this moment. I was becoming a Jew, and I was proud that I knew enough to enter into a conversation with these other scholars.

"I'd like you to tell us what this conversion means to you," Debbie, the woman on the Beit Din, said.

With that, tears slid down my face. "Everything," I answered, hardly able to speak.

The momentum of the questioning seemed to wind down, and Burt looked at his watch. "We'd better get to the *mikveh*, or else it will be closed," he said. Together we trooped down the hall, and by that time I felt light and full of laughter. I could have begun singing, so great was my relief, so great was my pleasure.

The *mikveh* is a ritual bath, large enough to cover the body of at least one person of average size, and containing water from a natural spring or a river. Many *mikvehs* are beautiful. I once saw one that was large enough for ten people, made of blue tiles and enclosed in a wood-paneled room with skylights and hanging plants, a place where I could happily lounge for hours.

But the *mikveh* at the synagogue that day was as bare-bones as it could be, a tiny hole in the concrete floor, dark and not very welcoming. "Hopefully they heated the water," Burt said, as we entered the room.

I hardly remember what happened next, except that I must have taken off my clothes in the changing room and quickly showered and shampooed my hair, since anyone entering the *mikveh* must be freshly clean. My nails clipped short, my body free of impediments, my long hair hanging down my back, I was ready for this final step in becoming a Jew.

Burt and the other man on the Beit Din stayed outside the room, beyond the cracked-open door, so that I could be naked without their seeing me. Debbie came into the room with me, my closest witness.

At this point I remember only the water: chilly, gray, not very appealing. But I was caught in the spirit of the moment, and I happily lowered myself into the four-foot depth, with Debbie standing above me.

"Ready?" Burt called.

"Yes," I called back.

"Okay, go ahead." I immersed myself totally in the water as I had been told, careful that my head was underneath. Cool water from the earth touched every surface of my body, and I was lost in the timelessness of those few seconds.

When I came up for air, I gasped. "Now say the first blessing," Burt said. Too excited to remember all the traditional words, I looked to Debbie for help: *"Baruch Ata Adonoy, Eloheinu melech ha-olam, asher kideshanu b'mitzvotav, vitzivanu al ha-tevillah."* In English, "Blessed are you, Lord our God, Creator of the universe who sanctified us through your commandments and taught us concerning immersion."

"Now go under the water again," Burt directed. Down I went, feeling great joy. This act was making me ritually clean, symbolizing my commitment to Judaism and my own rebirth.

When I emerged, I remembered to say the second traditional Hebrew blessing, the *Shehechiyanu,* "Blessed are you, Lord our God, Creator of the universe who has kept us alive and allowed us to reach this day."

Within my heart I said, "Thank you, thank you."

"Okay, one more time, and then you can get dressed," Burt called when I had finished. I inhaled deeply and went under the water, wanting to stay as long as I could. This was the transformative moment, when I would reemerge as a Jew.

I burst through the water when I no longer could hold my breath. *"Mazel tov!"* Debbie shouted, and I could hear the two men on the other side of the door yelling, *"Mazel tov! Mazel tov!"* Raising myself out of the *mikveh,* I wrapped myself in a towel. "Let me be the first to congratulate you," Debbie said, hugging me.

So this was it: the rebirthing I had looked forward to for months, years, decades. It wasn't much of an event, but the symbolism was staggering. A few dips in the water, a few blessings, and now I was a totally different person. I took my time dressing, dreamy, floating as though I were still in the *mikveh.*

In the room where the Beit Din had been held, Burt and the others were talking about a new Jewish school that was being organized. As I entered, they congratulated me again. "We'll wait a little for Michael," Burt said, and then they resumed their conversation.

No longer the center of attention, I listened to their shop talk until Michael arrived. "Here's a present," he said, handing me a crimson velvet pouch. Unzipping it, I found a beautiful *tallit,* a prayer shawl with stripes like a rainbow, that he had just bought at the Jewish bookstore. "The traffic was bad, that's why I didn't get here sooner," he apologized. "But I wanted you to have this right after your conversion." I couldn't imagine a more wonderful present from this man who had been such support through these long months.

Burt busied himself in the official paperwork for my conversion, a certificate in Hebrew that I could use in the future to prove that I was a Jew. This document would be the only record of what had just happened in the *mikveh*. "Your Hebrew name?" he asked. "I need it for the certificate."

I had been looking forward to this moment for a long time. "Nehama," I answered.

"Great choice! It suits you," Debbie said.

I nodded in agreement. Nehama, meaning comfort or compassion, was a name I had chosen carefully. I liked its sound and its meaning, but I wasn't sure. Only when I remembered that Nehama Leibowitz, the renowned biblical commentator, had this same name did I decide to take it as my own.

Nehama Leibowitz could have been my grandmother. Like Grandma Alice, she was a fiery old woman who loved her religion. I had discovered her books when I began studying Torah, and I decided that if anyone could be my namesake, it was this woman who had the intelligence and temerity to push her way into the ranks of male biblical commentators.

When Burt finished writing my Hebrew name on my certificate of conversion, he handed it to me. I glanced at this evidence of the most major change I had ever made in my life, and slipped it into my briefcase.

"And now, a short ceremony," he said. Opening a standard rabbinic book, he began to read a declaration of my Jewishness, with prayers and admonitions. My mind wandered. I was ready to let settle what had already happened.

When he finished, everyone gathered up their belongings. "Okay, that's it," I said to Michael. "Let's go." With thanks to Rabbi Burt and the others for their help, I left the synagogue, finally a Jew.

After my conversion I could have celebrated at one of the restaurants in town, or taken the rest of the afternoon off, but I was soon back at work.

This was a monumental day, but I did not mark it with festivities. The ritual at the *mikveh* had been private, an event unto itself. Although I felt deeply joyful, it had been a quiet joy, one that did not spread out to the world beyond the synagogue walls. The moments of connection with Rabbi Burt and the others on the Beit Din, the cool waters covering me, and Michael's appearance at the end of the conversion had been enough. Or so I thought.

But now I wonder. I intensely missed my children that day, wishing they were with me, wanting them to understand and accept what I was doing. And where was the community? Before the conversion Burt had said I could invite a few friends or family to the synagogue to welcome me as a Jew after I finished with the *mikveh,* but I had declined. It seemed too complicated, given the awkwardness in my life at that time.

Afterward, back in the office, I felt lonely. The day was anticlimatic. Although I didn't realize it then, the thrill of becoming Jewish demanded an outlet. Going to the *mikveh* had been like one hand clapping: to make the full sound I needed to celebrate with family and community. But I had cut them out.

I couldn't accept that becoming Jewish would cause me to be different from my children. When I spoke to my daughter early on the morning of my conversion, I mentioned that I was going to the *mikveh* that day. "It's just a little ceremony," I said. "No big deal."

I told her this, knowing that I was headed for one of the most profound experiences of my life and that it would have reverberations for her, too. In denying its importance, I was trying to reassure her, and myself, that I was still her mother, the one who loved her no matter what.

"You shall diligently teach [these words] to your children," the Torah instructs. The admonition to pass on knowledge about Judaism to the next generation is important enough to be repeated twice daily in prayer. But what about non-Jewish children? At the dinner table in Michael's and my house every night, Michael taught his Jewish son about the tradition. I at least could have told my daughter about the meaning of conversion or the reasons for the *mikveh*, but I was too afraid of us losing each other.

When something is denied, it casts a shadow. Perhaps it was appropriate for me to minimize my feelings about my conversion with my daughter, given the tenuousness in our relationship. But to do that I had to split myself off from her. And I had to split myself off from myself. Although I was emotionally present at the conversion, as I went about my work at the office afterward, I felt the result of this denial, faintly to be sure, but there nonetheless, in a feeling of unreality.

I also experienced an element of shame within me that day. When Burt suggested I invite others in the community to celebrate after the conversion, I could not think of anyone to ask. It wasn't that I didn't know people. There were several new friends I could have invited.

Shame kept me from doing it. These friendships were

based on me downplaying the fact that I wasn't yet a Jew. I had made them on Jewish ground, so to speak, and these friends knew me as a woman who led a Jewish life. If they came to my conversion, my Gentile background would pop into the center of their consciousness, and I was afraid that it would never recede.

That day, which even now I have trouble remembering, I took the easiest way out: I had a private conversion. I was righting something that was wrong, taking care of something that had gone undone too long. Herein lay the shame. Despite the joy of the occasion, despite the feeling of satisfaction, I was casting off a problematic identity. Like sneaking away for cosmetic surgery or going out of town to a drug treatment program, I was fixing myself, and I didn't want anyone to witness this.

Shame. Each of us carries our own special variety, shaped in childhood. Mine had its roots in my earliest years. When I was very young, I was an exuberant, uninhibited child, noisy and playful. I used to run, not walk, or so the family legend goes. But this life energy seemed to overwhelm my parents.

"Calm down," my mother said sternly.

"You should be ashamed of yourself," my father chastised.

Even though I was small, I came to believe that I was too much for them, too strong, too expressive, too wild. In an effort to appear otherwise, I learned to be secretive and careful, hiding my vitality, minimizing myself. I tried to be good. Taking my father's admonition to heart, I became ashamed when I wasn't.

As I grew older, I covered this feeling of shame with a certain righteous indignation. This was the only acceptable outlet I found for my anger.

"No, I'm not going to drive your fancy car," I'd say to my father as a teenager. "That's not who I am." The insistence on my own identity gave me pride and helped soothe the unresolved shame. I might not be acceptable to these parents, but I had my own integrity.

When I was in high school, in my churchgoing days, I developed a strong counterculture identity. This helped with the shame. Seeing myself as different from most other students, judging them to be superficial and materialistic, I didn't even try to fit in. I was committed to creating a better, more loving world, and conventional popularity wasn't my concern. Instead of making decorations for the school dance, I'd take the bus into San Francisco on Saturdays and head for the City Lights bookstore, where I'd buy poetry chapbooks and dream of a life away from the suburbs.

The seeds of shame had been implanted in me, but my sense of identity became a countervailing power. Growing into adulthood, I'd sometimes feel the old shame, but I'd remind myself of who I was and feel whole once again. A mother, a wife, a professional woman, a contributor to society, I was generally satisfied with the social space I occupied.

Thus it was surprising to me that shame became an issue when I converted to Judaism. In the past I had found solace from it in my identity, but now my identity was causing me shame. How had this happened? On the day of my conversion, at a time when I should have felt proud of myself, I was glad to get it over with, so that I no longer was a Gentile. My lack of celebration on that day revealed a certain grimness that accompanies an act of reparation.

We make choices to heal our wounds, I've discovered. In deciding to convert, I put myself in the position of having to confront my shame. Even though I had covered it up through the years, it had been there, haunting me, causing me to devalue myself. Once I was on my way to conversion, it flared up, unbidden.

That day of my conversion, when I hoped my Gentile background would fade into the distance, I had no idea I would take so long to make peace with my shame. Even now, I am still doing this work. Perhaps this feeling is stronger in me than in most other people, but I am not unique. We are all wounded in one way or another. Who among us doesn't carry shame? The questions we ask ourselves reveal it: Am I acceptable? Will I be loved if I am known in my fullness? Will my past be held against me?

Imagine joining a people who doesn't want converts. This is like pushing your way into the center of a gathering when you aren't even invited. It takes courage. I exaggerate here about the Jewish reception of converts, because the feeling is more layered and complex than pure disdain. But enough of this attitude exists so that it creates the possibility for converts to feel ashamed of themselves.

This was my experience, and I know I am not alone. The proof is that the act of conversion is so often done without involvement from the community. An arrangement has been made: the convert is expected to be silent about the event, and the community turns the other way so as to not embarrass the new Jew by noticing. Subtle as it may be, shame is inherent in the process.

Another facet of conversion reveals this shame. In traditional Judaism, converts are considered to be born anew at the moment of conversion, the *tabula* made *rasa* by immersion in the *mikveh*. What happened in the past no longer counts. All sins are forgiven.

The interpretation does not stop there. Gentile relatives are no longer considered related. Mothers, fathers, children, wiped off the slate like so much unwanted handwriting. Years of learning, years of growth, gone. In the place of our natural parents, we are given Avraham Avinu, father of all, and Sarah Imeinu, mother of all. In the place of the lost past, we are allowed the opportunity to make a Jewish life.

Nobody really thinks that converts are completely new people. Nor is it expected that we will completely reject our Gentile relatives. The Talmud instructs us to treat them kindly and respectfully. But we are encouraged to create a different, more distant relationship with these remnants from the non-Jewish past, taking care that we do not become ensnared in their ways.

Conversion requires becoming part of another culture and religion, so the argument goes. The psyche must be free to make the necessary new attachment. The possibility of seduction by non-Jews is so great that radical separation is necessary. If converts have other allegiances, the stability of the community is threatened.

For some converts, this break with the past is a great relief. I recently met a man who never got along with his parents. Still bitter, he wanted nothing more to do with them, and conversion was a good excuse. I do not feel comfortable with this construction of reality. How could I not claim my family as my own?

In recent years, as more people convert, the born-anew idea has come under question in the liberal branches of Judaism. I spoke recently with a reform rabbi who insists that converts reassure their non-Jewish families immediately after conversion that their relationship remains the same. And in Jewish renewal congregations, Gentile family members are often included in celebrations of conversions.

In the spirit of greater openness to converts' ties to the past, then, the idea of being born anew is occasionally revamped. It becomes a beautiful metaphor for the feeling of spiritual rebirth that accompanies conversion. Rather than expressing shamefulness and creating an immediate conflict of loyalties, it then honors the intensity of the conversion experience.

In the weeks that followed my conversion, the magazine took precedence over everything else. I was overwhelmed with the task of readying the first issue for the printer. Our office was strewn with paper and unfinished cups of tea, and our voices held a frazzled edge.

Even though the first issue of *Tikkun* was not yet in print, it appeared to be heading for success. We were receiving many daily letters from prospective subscribers and supporters, our phone lines were busy, and already authors were contacting us, wanting their work to appear in the magazine. The concept seemed to be catching on in a big way, to my relief.

Excited by this but concerned that the magazine meet everyone's expectations, we kept making last-minute changes. Articles were added, then dropped, then added again. I who had never designed anything before took on the task of creating the look of the magazine. Sketching out the cover, playing with colors and shapes, experimenting with typefaces, I depended on my intuition.

In those spring months, when I thought about my conversion, I was relieved that it was in the past. It had been a difficult chapter in my life, but now it was over. I no longer needed to worry.

Waking in the mornings, I'd remind myself that I was a Jew. But I still felt uncomfortable when I claimed my identity aloud. "Yes, I'm Jewish," I'd answer when people asked, but my internal voice said, "Are you sure?" When they didn't question me further, I felt that I had gotten away with something.

The phrase "we Jews" felt especially strange to me. Although I had gone to the *mikveh,* could I legitimately say I belonged to the Jewish people? The spiritual dimension of the conversion caused me no difficulty, but the ethnic part made me uneasy and self-conscious.

When I wrote the draft of my publisher's column for the first issue of *Tikkun,* I crossed out a sentence that began, "We, the Jewish people." In my mind it sounded too formal, but the deeper reason was that I didn't yet feel entitled to publicly make such a proclamation.

That spring a telephone call came from my father. This was a big event because he and I hardly spoke, even though we lived near each other.

My father had divorced my mother several years before, immediately marrying again. His new wife kept him from having contact with his previous family. We, his children and grandchildren, had been cast off like unwanted baggage, and this brought us pain. Why didn't he do something about this situation, we asked ourselves. His wife's pressure was the easiest explanation, but we could not ignore the message of rejection behind his passivity.

When the phone rang that day, I answered it with the usual, "*Tikkun,* may I help you?" On the other end of the line I heard only labored breathing. "Hello? Hello?" I called impatiently.

"Nan?" a voice finally said. "Is that you?"

I recognized him immediately. "Dad?" I replied, flooded with feeling. "What a surprise."

A long pause. "I hear you're Jewish."

"Yes, that's right." How he found out, I could not imagine. My mind raced with all the things I wanted to say, but I did not trust myself.

"The kids are okay?" he asked.

"Yes, they're fine." I gave him a brief rundown of colleges, jobs, and my daughter's marriage six months before.

Another pause before he spoke again. "Our dog Daisy's been sick. I have to feed her by hand."

"That's too bad," I replied. How could he speak of his dog when there was such disruption between us? For a moment my anger rose, but then my love for this man, and my sorrow in what had happened between us, caused my throat to constrict.

"You're okay, Pa?" I asked. "You know if you ever need anything, I'll be there. I miss you so much."

Again the long pause. "All religions are the same," he said, his voice so low I had to strain to hear his words. "Christian, Jew, whatever. It doesn't matter what you are."

With that, he abruptly hung up the telephone before I could say anything more, disappearing into the unfriendly territory of his own life.

I sat at the desk, weeping. We had spoken only a few minutes, and the unsaid words piled inside me, but I was deeply reassured by this conversation. I'd never know what my becoming Jewish meant to my father, because he would not reveal such thoughts. But he had given me his blessing: I had heard it in his voice, and felt it in his heart. This was something I had never expected.

"My father called," I said to Michael later that afternoon. "He seems to accept my conversion."

"That's good," Michael replied. "At least someone

does." His sarcasm came from his impatience with some members of my family for not accepting us more warmly.

"It takes a while," I said, reassuring myself as well as him.

My children supported me, but my mother, who still lived in the family home, was not pleased with my new life. It was bad enough that I was with Michael, who she did not understand, but I also had become a Jew.

When I had told her I was going to convert, she shook her head sadly. "I thought you used to like going to church."

"I did," I said, "but now I'm different." My attempts to explain why I was making this change did not help, and she began to tell me how she felt about my new religion. Shabbat was restrictive, but the worst was *kashrut,* the Jewish dietary laws. She could not grasp why anyone, much less her daughter, would follow this narrow-minded practice.

I knew that my mother's feelings about *kashrut* were connected to my turning down her food. No matter how gently I did it, I still was rejecting her, or so it seemed. Food and love were tied together in a primal way.

From my own experience as a mother, I understood this. I remembered my own hurt feelings when my teenage daughter refused my food, foraging through the refrigerator to cook for herself. But my mother's reaction surprised me even so, because I had lived decades away from her. Weren't we both too old for this kind of struggle?

I was torn between sympathy for my mother's discomfort and anger that I wasn't getting her approval. I wanted her to embrace me as a Jew, show interest in this new life, and appreciate the journey that led to it. When she didn't, I felt hurt.

With my father absent, my mother was now the head of the family. The strength within her that had been veiled in her earlier years was emerging in full force in her seventies. Sharp-witted and irrepressible, she could silence even the most confident member of the family with a tart remark.

Determined that the family remain together, she arranged for us to gather for holidays. These were always big events, as most of the relatives lived nearby: my sister and brother, in-laws, nieces and nephews, my own children, aunts and uncles. Over the years this family had become more culturally diverse. We now had Asian-American and gay members, and some of us had lived in other countries. My becoming Jewish should have been just one more stretch.

A few weeks after my conversion, my mother invited me for Easter. "You must come," she said. "We're having a honey-baked ham."

Food was the most obvious problem with this holiday celebration, although I could have brought my own or eaten just the vegetables, enduring her disapproval. But I was a new Jew, and didn't want to have anything to do with Easter. It was the most troublesome Christian holiday, with its imagery of Jesus on the cross and its accusation of Jewish responsibility. Even if I didn't go to church, the day had too many anti-Semitic associations. Besides, it came in the middle of my first Passover season as a Jew.

"I don't celebrate Easter now," I told my mother. "I'm not comfortable with it."

"What do you mean? You're part of the family."

"Yes, but it isn't my holiday anymore."

My mother's level of exasperation rose sharply. "Surely you're not going to reject your own family, are you?"

"Of course not," I answered guiltily. "It's just that I . . ." Realizing that nothing would make her feel better, I stopped. "I'll think about it," I ended.

Later I called to say that I'd drop by to see everyone on Easter, but wouldn't stay for dinner. I thought this was a creative compromise, but it didn't make her happy. "If that's all you can do . . ." she said.

My decision didn't make Michael happy, either. "Easter? You have to see your family on that day, of all days? Aren't you a Jew?"

"But I won't be celebrating," I replied. "And you don't have to come with me."

"How did I ever get involved with someone whose family is Christian?" he sighed.

In the end Michael accompanied me to my mother's house. All the relatives were there. At first the atmosphere was strained, as Michael was still a stranger, and his presence in my life bewildered them. We sat in the library having drinks, talking about travel, a neutral subject. But when it came time for them to eat their Easter dinner and us to leave, I didn't want to go. My desire to hold onto my family was stronger than usual, tinged as it was by a feeling of loss.

In the car on the way home, Michael and I began to talk about the gathering. "How was it for you?" I asked.

"If you like Easter eggs and little bunnies . . .", he laughed. But I knew that it had not been easy for him, either. This was not the warm, lively Jewish family he wished for himself.

Converts are pulled between two worlds, and those connected to them are also stretched. The discomfort I and everyone associated with me felt in those days after I converted is not unusual. I've heard stories more painful than mine, of parents disowning their converted children, of ruptures that never heal.

Fortunately I was spared the experience of being rejected by Michael's family. His son, who I loved, seemed to accept me without question, and his parents were openhearted toward me. But many converts are deeply hurt by the families of their Jewish partner. Upset that their offspring is not with a "real" Jew, worried about the ethnic fate of their unborn grandchildren, some parents wage warfare against the converted partner.

It takes years to get beyond this pain. The existing guides to conversion give short shrift to it. "Trouble with in-laws is not unusual," they say, but they do not describe the tears that are shed, the bitterness that is often carried for decades.

But relationships change over time. I know a converted woman whose Jewish in-laws refused to speak civilly to her at first. When she came to the family home for dinner with her new husband, they ignored her, remarking disparagingly about the *goyim* they had known. Stung by this reception, she stayed away, but eventually, after a child was born, these Jewish relatives made overtures toward her, indirectly apologizing.

Even if conversion is a private act, it touches the lives of everyone connected to it. Like the stone thrown into the pond, its effects ripple outward. The family members closest to the convert feel it the most, but distant members are not excluded. My niece, who I hardly know, now has a Jewish aunt, and this cannot help but make a difference in how she views herself. "Jewish" will never again be entirely "other."

After my conversion I tried to hold steady in the rippling water of family reactions, but it was difficult. Every relationship seemed precarious. I had done something so immense that I couldn't rely on my family's natural good-will and elasticity. Scared that I would lose them, I began to withdraw in self-protection. My decision to leave my mother's house before Easter dinner was only the first step. I was busy, after all, with my new Jewish life.

Something was changing within me faster than I could grasp. Now that I had crossed over the ethnic line, I was beginning to see through Jewish eyes. Nobody could have told me beforehand what this was like.

One evening an old friend of mine from childhood came over. It had been a decade since we were last together. Exchanging news about people we knew, telling each other about our lives, the conversation flowed as it had in the past. Together we made a meal of salmon, new potatoes, and tomato salad.

When the food was ready, we settled around the big table in the dining room. As usual, Michael held up a loaf of bread and said the Hebrew blessing, breaking off chunks and handing them to us after we said, "Amen." In that moment I became self-conscious. What did my friend think? The Hebrew words, the pulling apart of the bread, the shared moment of appreciation were now a natural part of my life, but to her they must have seemed strange.

I looked around the room, noticing everything through her eyes. The poster on the wall commemorating the 1948 victory in Israel, the Jewish ritual objects on the shelf, the Jewish books piled in the corner. Everything Jewish. And I, her old friend who she had known in an entirely different context, was a part of this way of life, acting as if it was entirely normal.

The table conversation drifted along, more awkward now that there were three of us. "The magazine is getting a lot of attention," I said, but as the words came out of my mouth, I knew that the meaning eluded her, because she understood nothing about the complexities of Jewish culture or Jewish life. How could she? Certainly I hadn't, before I began to work on the magazine and before I converted.

"That's nice," she replied in a lukewarm way, without asking more. I felt myself become irritated with her. What a *goy*, I thought. Lacking in interest and energy. Constrained by Christian manners. I was beginning to develop a hint of disdain toward those not Jewish.

When my friend spoke about her life, it seemed distant and unreal to me, even though we both came from the same cultural background. I judged it harshly, assigning it less value than the Jewish life I was leading.

But then I began to feel sad at the loss of connection between us, realizing that the gulf was now very wide. When we did the *Birkat HaMazon*, the grace after the meal that lasts a good ten minutes, I anxiously checked her for signs of restlessness. Usually Michael and I accompanied the last prayer by pounding on the table in time to the music, and tonight was no exception. Although she smiled at our show of enthusiasm, I felt shy and embarrassed in her presence.

It was late when my friend left. "Did you enjoy yourself?" Michael asked, as we scraped the dishes and put them in the dishwasher together. "Yes, but it wasn't the same," I answered, too tired, too confused, too sad to give him a more complete explanation.

From what vantage point was I seeing the world? Increasingly in the months following my conversion I located myself within the Jewish sphere. Gentiles were different, and in some ways not as good as those of us within this sphere. Yet with provocation, or even without it, I'd switch back into seeing Jews as I had before, when I was firmly rooted in the non-Jewish culture. Then I was the outsider looking in, perceiving Jews as other than myself, confusing and strange.

This double vision often felt schizophrenic. I ping-ponged back and forth in a way that seemed out of control, worrying when I momentarily forgot that I was now a Jew. Did this mean that I hadn't really converted in my heart? Or that I was secretly disloyal?

My growing attitude of disdain toward non-Jews concerned me. The nightmare, the worst fantasy of all, was that my feelings toward my own children would be affected. If I were to reject them because of their ethnic background, what kind of person was I? Such an idea was not only ironic but horrifying. When my children came over, I examined myself carefully for signs of disdain, relieved to find that it was not there.

I was in a state of great unsettledness. But how could it have been otherwise? The dip in the *mikveh,* although symbolically important, did not wipe out my history or transform my perception. It didn't help me figure out my relationship to Jews and Gentiles. Years would go by before my identity more fully congealed.

Meanwhile, I had a dream one night. My body was stained with big patches of blue and red. In some places the colors swirled together, like colors on a pallet. I could hardly believe the sight.

Rubbing myself, I found that the colors went deeper than my skin. At first I was alarmed, but I became so engrossed in the intricacies of design that it didn't seem to matter, and the dream drifted elsewhere.

I do not like the word *convert*. Its sound is heavy and ungraceful. A close cousin in tone to *convict* and *contract,* it lacks a poetic ring. When I compare my experience as a convert to the word itself, it does not begin to hold the depth of my feeling.

Before I converted, I looked up the word *convert* in *Webster's* dictionary, and found it defined as "one who has adopted a religion." This is not an accurate description for those of us who have converted to Judaism, because it leaves out ethnicity. The word seems pale, more Christian than Jewish.

As much as I don't like the word, however, it is better than *Jew-by-choice,* which is favored in reform Judaism. That term is even more awkward and cumbersome, and I seldom use it. To say that I converted, I'd have to triple the number of words and report that I became a Jew-by-choice. A manuscript on this subject becomes dotted with hyphens.

The confusion that has been generated by *Jew-by-choice* is enormous, because all Jews conceivably fall into that category. Jewish identity bestowed at birth can be discarded, and a choice must be made, however unconscious, for it to remain.

The label *Jew-by-choice* raises the ire of many people. At a recent gathering in California I was approached by a Jewish woman who knew that I was a convert: "Why do you call yourselves Jews-by-choice?" she asked. "It doesn't fit you any more than it does me."

"Nobody's trying to take something from you," I replied. "It's just a way of getting past the negative baggage that comes with the word *convert*."

With that, she seemed to soften. "Okay, but I still don't like it."

When *Jew-by-choice* was coined over a decade ago, it seemed to be a positive solution to the disapproval inherent in the word *convert,* and it has caught on in some circles. As well intentioned as it is, however, it creates confusion.

"This is Nan, a con-" one man recently began. "I mean a Jew-by-choice. Or should I say convert?" he ended. In an attempt to not embarrass me, he couldn't find quite the right label.

I am reminded of the difficulty that exists with racial designations. Should we say black or African-American? American Indian or Native American? In fact, people who are white don't worry about embarrassing people by calling them white, because they do not consider it a disparaging term. They are concerned with offending minority groups by using the wrong name. Likewise, Jews don't think twice about calling someone else a Jew, but they worry about having the right name for converts. The concern about names reveals their uneasiness with us.

When I went to the library to begin my research about conversion several years ago, I first checked in the computer under "convert" and "Jew-by-choice." To my surprise there were no listings, and I was instructed to search under "proselyte."

Proselyte? I had never heard that word used before for converts, although I soon learned that it has been a common designation throughout Jewish history. When I looked up its definition, I found that it means "a new convert; specif: a convert to Judaism." Now I was getting somewhere. A name that refers to Judaism. Furthermore, it derives from the Greek word *proselytos,* which is defined as "resident alien."

In Hebrew the word for convert, *ger,* has the same meaning. This connection holds the history of the word: from Hebrew to Greek, from Greek to English, a trip from ancient times to the present.

For a while I thought about using *proselyte* to describe myself, but soon abandoned it. I like its sound less than *convert,* and it is unfamiliar to most American Jews. More importantly, its verb form in contemporary English goes against the Jewish grain, as fundamentalist Christians are the ones who proselytize, while Jews are appalled at the idea.

Rather than adopting *proselyte,* with its Christian-associated verb form, I began to consider the Hebrew word *ger.* Why not use this more authentic word, which has its roots in biblical times? Known by all Hebrew speakers, it appears frequently in the Torah. But as I began to explore this possibility, I found that it, too, wouldn't work.

In my Hebrew-English dictionary, *ger* is translated as "foreigner; stranger; resident alien." Three meanings in one word. This does not present a problem in English, because these meanings are distinct from each other, with separate definitions. But in Hebrew a great confusion exists.

When one is reading the Torah and comes across the word *ger,* it can signify any or all of the meanings in the definition. Nobody tries to sort them out. As a result, *convert* is conflated with *stranger* and *resident alien.* This exists in modern Hebrew, as well as in biblical Hebrew.

Did I want to use a word that forever marked me as a

stranger or resident alien? The answer was no. As beautiful as *ger* sounded, and as much as I wished to use Hebrew, I could not ignore the meaning of the word. Nor could I deny that it made me feel unknown, uncared for, and a second-class citizen.

Embedded in this word was too much difficulty. It revealed the heart of the convert's dilemma, the pain of joining but not being fully accepted. In its favor, it truthfully represents the attitude toward converts, because it doesn't pretend to consider us in a flattering light. But words shape reality, as well as reflect it, and this word perpetuates a certain negative image of converts.

And so it is back to *convert,* that workhorse of a word. It will have to do until a better one emerges. "I am a convert," I now say when people ask. I try to feel pride in the word, but it disappoints me, and my feeling of strength comes not from the word but from within myself.

In the spring after my conversion I seldom referred to myself as a convert. Even in my own mind I dropped the label. I was a Jew, and that's what counted.

The people at the orthodox shul were oblivious to the fact that I had finally converted. Sometimes I imagined announcing it at the end of the service when the president of the congregation asked for congregational news, but I didn't dare. Nobody would have approved, as mine had been a conservative conversion.

Still, my relationship to the shul began to change. A few of the congregants now greeted me after Saturday morning services. Time was taking its course. Rather than fleeing from the room after the congregational announcements were over, I'd go up to these people at the *kiddush* table, ignoring the others who refused to speak.

"You've been treated poorly," a woman who had a son the same age as Michael's, confided. "It shouldn't have happened. I'm sorry."

As she said this, I felt my bitterness rise. "It's been horrible," I replied. No apologetic, mediating remarks from me that day.

Although I was pleased to find support, I cared little about the orthodox shul by that time. I had given up on it, but also I had other things on my mind. With the publication date of the magazine coming so soon, I could hardly think of anything else. In the tree-house office, Michael and I worked longer and longer hours that spring, putting the final touches on the first issue.

By this time our life together had fallen into a certain pattern. All week we'd strain to get everything done before Shabbat, then on Friday afternoon, at the very last minute, we'd rush home, stopping at the grocery to pick up supplies. Flying into the kitchen, we'd cook ahead for the next twenty-four hours. Soup and salad, baked chicken, yams and applesauce for dinner, and vegetable *cholent* or lasagna for the next day's lunch. Sometimes I'd think how strange it was to be in such a frenzy to get ready for a day of rest.

Shabbat preparations had their own rhythm, and once the table was set and the house straightened, the pace began to slow. "It's your turn first in the shower," I'd call to Michael. "Okay, but it's getting late," he'd answer, concerned about starting Shabbat at sunset.

In the bathroom I'd linger at the mirror, examining myself, stroking the little lines on my face, taking as much time as I could to settle into a mood of quietness. When I joined Michael and his son for the lighting of the candles, the whole house seemed transformed. Papers and books were neatly piled, flowers stood in a vase on the table, and the golden light of the setting sun filled the room.

I carefully lit the two Shabbat candles on the mantle, drawing the light toward myself. Covering my eyes, I chanted the age-old Hebrew blessing, *"Baruch Ata Adonoi, Eloheinu melech ha-olam . . . l'hadlik ner shel Shabbat."* In English, "Blessed is God, the creator of the universe, who commands us to kindle the light of Shabbat." The room felt strangely peaceful, and the tightness in my body began to dissolve, the candlelight warming every part.

Shabbat is like nothing else. Time as we know it does not exist during these twenty-four hours, and the worries of the week soon fall away. A feeling of joy appears. The smallest object, a leaf or a spoon, shimmers in a soft light, and the heart opens. Shabbat is a meditation of unbelievable beauty.

Sitting together on the couch, we'd begin to sing the psalms and prayers that make up the evening service. By then, I had learned most of the words, or at least could follow along, and I was soon enveloped in a sweet peace. Michael would rock back and forth, radiant, then every so often prod his son to keep on singing.

When I think of what was best in that home, I think of Shabbat. Afterward, after I left, I'd yearn for these moments. The tight circle we made when the service was over, arms wrapped around each other, singing *"Shalom Aleichem."* The jokes afterward about our eardrums breaking because we had sung so loud. The warmth between Michael and me, and the sweetness with his son.

And then the meal. How can anyone know how sensual food tastes after all this? Like lovemaking after glances and sighs. The challah with honey, the yam's smooth interior, the tomato, the cucumber. On it went, so that we were surfeited with pleasure.

The next morning we'd usually hike down the hill to the orthodox shul. In our fancy dress we'd pass by people pruning their trees or washing their cars. I was different, set apart by the way I looked and the way I lived. Wrapped in a Shabbat consciousness, I found the rest of the world most peculiar, and I could hardly believe I hadn't noticed before.

After the services it was back up the hill, a climb that took an hour and a half. When we finally arrived at the house, lunch went on the table, the thick vegetable *cholent* with challah and cheese, or the lasagna with salad left over from the night before. Each meal of Shabbat is accompanied by songs and discussion, and even though the week's exhaustion seemed to hit about this time and I could hardly wait to go upstairs for a nap, we lingered around the table.

The most tender moments of Shabbat are in the late afternoon. These precious final hours of Shabbat are quiet and mellow, and a little sad because the day is slipping away. We'd lie around and read, or study together, or Michael and his son would play chess while I daydreamed. And then, when we counted three stars in the darkening sky, we'd go outside to do *Havdalah*, the service that separates Shabbat from everyday life. *"Shavuah tov,"* we'd say to each other afterward. "Have a good week."

I write here about Shabbat because it was the center of my life, and still is, even though my observance of it is no longer as circumscribed. I once met a woman who told me that Shabbat was the most important thing she did all week. "My job, and the rest of it, are nothing in comparison," she said. The pleasure she took in anticipating Friday night kept her going.

That spring, in the anxious flurry about *Tikkun,* I experienced Shabbat like an anchor. Forcing me to rest, helping me to have a wider view of life, it was a bit of sanity in what was beginning to feel like a too-fast life. I had not bargained for such a demanding schedule, but I didn't know how to contain it, except by Shabbat.

Still, my level of excitement about the magazine remained. In May we placed our first advertisement in the *New York Times.* "Finally, a liberal alternative to *Commentary,*" it read. The subscriptions began to pour in, and we received some letters of condemnation because of our provocative position. We were on our way to becoming visible, although it was hard to imagine in the hideaway office, nestled in the California hills.

On a Friday afternoon late in May, Michael and I waited alone on the redwood deck for the shipment of our first issue of the magazine to arrive. We had gone through the terrors of typesetting and paste-up, and soon we would see the results of all our efforts.

Already the shadows were lengthening. "We can't stay any longer," Michael said. "Shabbat starts in an hour." But I insisted on waiting, as it would have been hard to settle into Shabbat with this on our minds.

Finally a truck horn blasted on the street, and a few minutes later the driver stomped up our long dirt driveway, complaining that our office was too far from the road. In his truck were forty-six boxes of magazines, and he had no one to help him, so we rushed down and loaded the wheelbarrow, dragging it over the potholes in the driveway, back and forth, until all the boxes were in a pile inside the house.

When the driver left, I carefully opened the first box. There, purple and gold, Volume I, Number 1, was our magazine. My heart was racing.

"Oh, no, it's ugly!" I moaned. Pulling a copy out, I began to leaf through it. "A typo! How could we have missed it? It's right here, in the most important place."

"Enough," Michael said. "We've got to get home for Shabbat."

I closed the magazine, and marched out the door. I didn't ever want to see that issue again. Little did I know that in the future I would go through this same reaction every time a new issue arrived. Sometimes it would take me days to pick it up, so great was my fear of finding mistakes.

Before the arrival of the first issue of the magazine, we had been intent on its production. But afterward a whole new set of tasks became apparent. We had printed 40,000 magazines and we had only a few hundred subscribers. Should we give the rest away or keep them to sell? The next issue of the magazine loomed before us, with its blank pages to be filled. Like new parents who are shocked by the way an infant takes over their lives, we could hardly believe how much work was generated by this first issue.

Not anticipating this, we had made a plan for the upcoming summer. We would stay in California until the shipment of magazines arrived, then fly to Jerusalem, where Michael would direct a summer program in peace studies. The year before, while I had been at the women's yeshivah, he had organized this program.

Our plan was unrealistic, but the program in Israel was already set up. There was nothing to do but go once again to Jerusalem and leave the magazine in the hands of our assistant, who would take care of the mail and await our calls of instruction. I considered staying in California by myself but decided against it, as I was not sure my relationship with Michael would withstand such a long absence.

On our way to Israel, we'd stop in New York, we decided. With the first issue in hand, this was a good opportunity to introduce the magazine to the East Coast media. Michael, who was skilled in promotion, volunteered to put together a few press kits and send them out before we left California. Perhaps someone would be interested.

The response to our homemade press kits was far more enthusiastic than I expected. "*Newsweek* wants an interview," Michael said. "They're doing an article on Norman Podhoretz and me. And I've got interviews with a few other top-notch publications."

"Great!" I answered. This was good news for the magazine, and could only help our circulation. But as pleased as I was, I felt envious. Michael, it seemed, was now emerging as the spokesperson for the magazine. I was in danger of being left behind. I could accompany him on these interviews if I wished, he reassured me, but I had not been invited and the thought made me uncomfortable.

Somehow I had not anticipated this development during the months of creating the magazine. I had gotten caught up in the notion of us acting as one creative mind. Unprepared for how the world would see us, I was shocked at how quickly we diverged in our public roles.

The interest in Michael was hardly surprising, however. *Newsweek* deemed a potential dispute between two male intellectuals worthy of attention. Where could a woman fit in? This was the male world, with all its battles for power. I realized it would be nearly impossible for me to be included in the drama. Besides, I was a newly converted Jew, without the background or confidence to be an articulate spokesperson for Jewish issues at that time.

This realization depressed me far more than I allowed. In the past I had worked hard to have my own career. I never wanted to be the woman-behind-the-scenes, but now it seemed that this was happening. How could I change it?

"You'll find a place for youself," Michael argued. "There's enough room for us both. Concentrate on the issues that concern you, and you'll make an important contribution."

"I'll give it a try," I said, although his advice seemed beyond my reach. With all the responsibilities and administrative details of publishing the magazine, I could not imagine where I'd find the energy or the time.

When I arrived at the Ben Gurion airport in Israel that summer, I bent down and kissed the ground, as is the custom, but I did not feel the excitement of the past year. Michael and I settled into an apartment in Jerusalem's German Colony, a neighborhood with leafy trees and big Arab houses. This apartment was more luxurious than the one we had rented before, with large rooms and paintings on the walls, but I continued to feel depressed.

Michael rushed from meeting to meeting while I sat despondently in the garden in a green lawn chair, reviewing my life. I had come this far, and was now the publisher of a magazine that promised to be successful. But who was I, anyhow? A Jew, that was certain. But being Jewish wasn't what I thought it would be. In the past I had hoped that I would feel included in the Jewish community after my conversion, but now I saw that I had been naive. As a convert, I was just as insecure, maybe even more so.

Not only that, but I was discovering the difficulties of being a Jewish woman. Gender was far more entrenched in this world than I had realized. I had seen it operating in orthodoxy, and now I was getting a glimpse of it in the political, organizational sphere. What hope did I have? As a

woman for whom sexual equality had always been a matter of principle, I was chagrined that I had gotten myself
into this situation.

Discouraged, I tried to convince myself that I was just
going through a stage. After my conversion and the excitement of creating the magazine, an emotional crash was
predictable. I had become a Jew for the long haul, and I
needed to accept the hard times with the good times, the
imperfect with the perfect.

I told myself that I was being too reactive, too hard on
Michael, too hard on myself. My feelings were undoubtedly heightened by an envy that was left over from my
childhood. My younger brother had commanded more attention with his brilliance and his emotional need, and now
I was plunged into a replay of the past, with Michael flour-
ishing and me floundering. I reminded myself that I was an
adult, not a sad, older sister, and that I should marshal my
resources to handle this situation.

Back and forth I swung. In my lawn chair I tried to
summon the energy to begin an article, or organize the Israeli promotion for the magazine, but I felt paralyzed. The
summer before had been filled with exploration, but this
summer I accomplished hardly anything, which made me
feel only worse. I couldn't even relax enough to take the
time as a vacation. When people dropped by, I smiled and
served drinks, but I was hardly interested in the conversation. Only on Shabbat did I find relief, as I sank into the
peace of the day.

One experience in particular summed up my unhappiness that summer. The *Jerusalem Post,* an English-language
newspaper, wanted to do an article about *Tikkun,* and this
time I went along with Michael to the office, where we
were interviewed by a seasoned editor.

"Why did you create the magazine?" the man asked. Michael spun off several reasons, concentrating on his concern about the political situation in Israel. I seconded him, and offered a few reasons of my own, but I was unsure of myself in this setting, and felt like an imposter when I voiced concerns about the American Jewish world.

The interview went on for some time, with questions about the philosophy of the magazine. I became increasingly quiet. Finally the editor wanted to know about our backgrounds. Michael answered first, describing his Jewish education and his dedication to Judaism from a young age.

When it was my turn, I talked about my professional background. "And your Jewish training?" the man asked, after listening patiently.

This was the moment I had been dreading. Although I could have sidestepped the question, I had the sudden impulse to tell him the truth. "I'm a convert," I said. "But I've studied Judaism for many years. Last summer I was in Jerusalem taking courses at Mikhlelet Bruria."

"I see," he replied. For a moment he sat quietly, looking down, then he raised his dark eyes to mine. "I won't say anything about your conversion. Nobody will know, I promise you."

He was doing me a favor, since the legitimacy of *Tikkun* might suffer if it were publicized that I was a convert. I understood this, but I felt a sudden stiffening of will. "Thanks," I said. "But you can include this information in the article."

He waved away the idea. "No, I wouldn't do that."

I wanted to fight him at that moment. I wanted to insist that he tell everyone about my conversion and get it over with, once and for all. I yearned to have it known that I, a convert, could create something of value. The pressure that had been building within me all summer almost exploded that day.

"Include it, please," I said in a firm tone. "I really want you to."

But that was the end of the discussion, and we were quickly ushered out of the office. When the article appeared in the *Jerusalem Post* a few days later, I scanned it to see if my secret had been revealed. It was no surprise that it hadn't.

Jerusalem, the city where everything comes to the surface. That summer I could barely contain my contradictory feelings. More than any time there, I threatened to split apart. If I could have spoken to someone who had navigated these difficulties, I might have been reassured. But Michael and my Israeli friends had all been born Jewish, and they would not have understood.

The only time I felt steady that summer was when my college-age son came to visit. His presence reassured me. I had spent the summer in a bad state, but I was still a mother; this was something that couldn't be taken away. As I showed him around Jerusalem, his excitement about what he was learning cheered me up. A connection between my new life and my children seemed possible, after all.

Before I returned to California, I went alone to the Western Wall. This was not something I often did that summer, as it was clear across town. Climbing down the steps through the Old City, I saw the wall's rough surface and felt a rush of anticipation. It was late afternoon, the time for *minchah,* the second prayer service of the day, and for once there was no crowd.

The wall was like a magnet, drawing me in. Faster and faster I went, no longer willing to wait, and I flung myself at it, pressing my body against the ancient stones. My tears began to flow.

The summer had been too painful, too hard. I remembered the year before, my joy in becoming a Jew and the pleasure I had taken in learning. My spirit had soured since then, for reasons I hardly understood and did not want to accept. Where did this leave me?

Leaning against the wall close by, an old woman wept. Perhaps she was mourning a death. I, too, had a death, although my death was of a dream that I had carried for so long. No more could I believe that becoming a Jew would be sweet and easy.

Above me the huge stones towered, chiseled millennia ago by the Herodians. A small swallow landed on a vine growing from one of these stones, then flew away. Next to me a young woman in orthodox dress swayed, feet together, reciting *minchah;* then she, too, leaned against the wall and began to sob, clutching her prayer book to her breast.

My pain sharpened. All the losses of my past came before me, and joined the death of my dream. I was filled with the sound of the women around me grieving, all our pain, all one.

And then the sound ebbed. The young orthodox woman backed away from the wall, closing her prayer book. The old woman tightened the scarf around her head, kissed the spot where she had wept, and walked stiffly away. I silently said goodbye to them.

I fingered the cracks between the stones, crammed with hundreds of tiny notes written by the women who had been there before me. Taking my pen from my purse and tearing a slip of paper from my notebook, I wrote a note, underlining each word. *"Give me the strength,"* it said.

I rolled up the note, kissed it, then pushed it gently into a crack. With that, I felt a sense of great relief. It would be all right. The summer had shown me the dark side, and I had descended into it, but I would emerge.

Already the sky was beginning to shade with evening. Looking at my watch, I saw that I had been at the wall for almost three hours. Suddenly I was more thirsty than I had been all summer. Turning my back on those stones that had absorbed so much feeling, I headed toward a small cafe.

I did not realize how pivotal that second summer in Israel was until I arrived home. "How was your trip?" my oldest daughter asked.

"Really hard," I answered, describing some of my unhappy moments. I felt more open to her, not as concerned about proving that I had made the right choice. My son's visit to Israel had made me feel less afraid of losing her, but I had also found a willingness within myself to acknowledge the difficulties of conversion.

In the *Tikkun* office the work had piled high in our absence. I plowed right in. Here I was needed, my contribution valuable with dozens of manuscripts to read, calls to make, the next issue of the magazine to organize.

One early autumn evening I cruised along the freeway on my way home from work, singing with the Israeli tape on my tape deck. My voice was lighter and more expressive than it had been in several months. I was feeling better: something within me had shifted, and I had more energy and felt more alive.

This different state was tinged with something new, a feeling of assertion. Even if being Jewish was difficult, even if it touched on some deep pain, I was going to make it work for me. With all the determination that had served me well in the past, I knew that I would fight to have the best experience possible.

"I'm not going to shul with you," I told Michael one Shabbat.

"Why?" he asked.

"Because I'm not comfortable there." A simple statement, but it had taken me a long time to be so straightforward.

"So we'll stay home," he answered.

As the weeks of the fall went by, Michael and I seldom hiked down the hill to the orthodox shul. The sweetness of these Saturday mornings at home, *davvening* the morning service, pleased me. When we read the Torah portion aloud, we would take time to discuss a verse at length or stop when it seemed right, rather than push through to the end.

One Saturday morning a noted rabbi was giving the sermon at the shul, and I decided to go. Entering the building after a few months' absence, I saw the room through different eyes. There, on one side, were the men, and on the other, the women. An arrangement coming from sexism and men's fear of women, no matter how it was explained. How could I have spent so long in a place like this?

At the end of the morning service, the winners of the yearly Hebrew school essay contest were announced, a boy and a girl who were going to read their entries on a subject I no longer remember. The boy proudly stood on the *bimah,* the special platform in the center of the room where the men led the prayers. He spoke with an air of confidence. When it was the girl's turn, she read her paper from the floor in front of the women's section, as she was not allowed on the *bimah*. From this position her thin voice was hard to hear, her face impossible to see.

In that moment the split parts of myself fused. My concern about feminism no longer could be cut off from my religious life. Even though I resonated spiritually with the orthodox service, even though I was attracted to an observant way of life, I could not continue to support a structure that diminished women.

Walking up the hill afterward with Michael and an orthodox woman who lived close by our house, I fumed. "That was too much," I said to the neighbor, who I hardly knew.

"What do you mean?"

"That girl not being able to read from the *bimah*."

"Her essay was better than the boy's," the woman said carefully. "Standing on the *bimah* really isn't so important."

"But think what that girl is learning about herself," I retorted. "No matter how smart she is, she'll never get the validation that boy gets!" My walking partner just shrugged.

I couldn't get the subject out of my mind. Later at the lunch table, I brought it up again with Michael and his son. "That girl was treated poorly," I said. They both agreed, although they did not share the depth of my distress. I was on fire, wanting to change that shul, protect that girl, and shake everybody loose.

"Sexism!" I said loudly. "There's too much sexism in Judaism. It's absolutely not right!" This was not a new truth, but I hadn't allowed myself to care so much about it before. No longer the non-Jew looking in, no longer the one who appreciated everything about Judaism, I was claiming my right to criticize: I didn't like what I saw, and I wasn't going to keep quiet.

As the fall went by, this feeling of distress about sexism extended further. I increasingly noticed it in Jewish organizations. As the publisher of a national magazine, I often went to conferences and meetings that I, a new convert, ordinarily would not have attended. There I kept a stern observer's eye.

At a Jewish Federation meeting of young profession-als on the East Coast, I noticed with irritation that the men seemed to dominate every meeting. In one session, sixteen men spoke before a woman finally got the microphone, and once she started to make her point, they became rest-less, hardly listening.

"This is terrible," I wrote in my notes. "There's more sexism in these organizations than I've ever seen." An ex-aggeration, to be sure, but I was allowing myself to ac-knowledge even more the shadow side of this world I had embraced.

In the past I had been aware of sexism, but I'd not been so reactive. Like other women, my life was shaped by gender and I was groomed to be a nurturing caretaker. This had made me angry all along, but I hadn't fully ac-knowledged it. It took becoming a Jew to make me less complacent.

Sexism was not the only issue that bothered me that fall. I began to take on the cause of converts. I had been affected by the ambivalent attitude among Jews toward converts all along, but now I became even more disturbed.

One day I stopped by the print shop to pick up an or-der of flyers for the magazine. There I saw a familiar-look-ing man, who reminded me that we had been introduced at a recent lecture. We chatted for a few moments, then he said, "I hear you've converted."

"Yes," I answered, surprised that he spoke so freely. Most Jews don't bring up the subject.

"I don't get it," he said. "You had it made as a Chris-tian. What could you possibly achieve by becoming a Jew? The Jewish religion is archaic and irrelevant."

I started to answer, but he continued. "And now you

have to deal with anti-Semitism. Why would anyone in their right mind take that on?"

This man's attitude irritated me. If I had known him, I might have taken the time to explain myself, but I didn't want to fight with a stranger. "Judaism satisfies me," I answered shortly, turning away.

That stopped him, but I was left with the feeling of having been judged. It wasn't the first time, and it certainly wasn't the last. Hardly a week goes by without someone making a comment like this, once they find out I'm a convert.

Many secular Jews cannot grasp why I would want to convert, because they themselves don't find meaning in Judaism. Their ethnic identity has been a burden all their lives, and they've tried to escape it, so something must be wrong with one who chooses it.

It is frequently said that secular Jews are more disparaging of converts than observant Jews. Observant Jews at least understand the attraction of Judaism. But my experience in the religious community showed me that these people judge converts as unkindly as secular Jews. Their rejection comes from fear and suspicion, rather than misunderstanding, but it is just as potent.

That fall, when I was especially disturbed about the attitude of Jews toward converts, I began an investigation. I remembered from my preconversion reading that converts were treated differently in other historical times. Perhaps if I researched the subject, I would learn something about the past that would make being a present-day convert easier.

I took several books on Jewish history out of the library. During the biblical era, before 400 B.C.E., large numbers of non-Jews joined the Israelites, I discovered. Many of them already lived within the borders of Israel. Intermarriage was extremely common then, and there was no formal ritual of conversion, as the religion itself was evolving.

The boundaries of the Jewish people were at their most porous during that time. I found myself envying the ease in which someone could become Jewish. This ease, however, belied a problem of status. Although converts were considered to be Jews, they were still *gerim,* strangers in the land, different from born-Jews, and not allowed to hold some public offices.

During the latter part of the Second Temple period, 300 B.C.E. to 70 C.E., Israelites began to travel to other lands and spread the word about Judaism. More people converted. The attitude toward conversion was still positive, but the ethnic boundaries were tightening. These new converts were never accepted as being fully Jewish: they were considered part of the Jewish religious fellowship, but not part of the Jewish race or nation.

After the fall of the Second Temple in 70 C.E. and the dispersal of the Jews, conversion increased for several centuries. There is even some report of missionary activity. Conversion was seen by some as a way to ensure the continuation of the Jewish people.

Conversion was so common that the Talmud—written from 200 to 500 C.E.—dealt with it in depth. From the writings we can see the mixture of feelings that existed then toward converts. On the positive side, the Talmud says: "God dealt kindly with Israel in scattering them among the nations, for, because of this, *gerim* were added to Israel." The fall of the Second Temple was a tragedy, but it was also a blessing, because more people were drawn to Judaism.

And: "The *ger* is dearer to God than Israel was when the nation assembled at the foot of Mt. Sinai. For Israel would not have accepted the Torah without seeing the thunder and lightning and the quaking mountain and hearing the sound of the *shofar,* whereas the proselyte, without a single miracle, consecrates himself to the Holy One. . . . "

As I read these passages from the Talmud, I was moved by the respect expressed for people like myself. Even in those ancient times, we were seen as contributing something of value.

But the Talmud also reveals a countervailing opinion: "Converts are as troublesome to Israel as a leprous sore."

And "Evil after evil comes on those who receive converts."

This negativity sounded familiar, although the language is stronger than any I've heard in my lifetime. Perhaps the experience of being a convert was not so different in the past. Scholars point out that these negative passages in the Talmud can be interpreted in many ways, but the impression remains that they reveal an unfavorable attitude toward converts.

After the Talmudic period ended, persecution against the Jews increased in the Diaspora and conversion became dangerous. In the Middle Ages this danger intensified. Rabbis were killed for performing conversions, Jewish communities were severely persecuted if they took in non-Jews, and converts were sentenced to death. Still, the practice continued.

I was especially fascinated by the difficulty of conversion in this historical period. One story in particular haunted me, that of Nicholas Antoine, a man born in early-sixteenth-century Lorraine. Like me, he was a Protestant. When he was young, he, too, had a passion for religion.

I had become a minister's wife, but Nicholas Antoine went to a Christian seminary to study for the ministry. This was expected of him, as he came from a family that produced clergymen. However, he had a revelation during his studies, and decided he really wanted to be a Jew.

Leaving the seminary, he wandered throughout France and Italy for several months, looking for a rabbi to convert him. None would, because it was too dangerous. Discouraged, he returned to the seminary where he secretly taught himself the Hebrew prayers and recited them morning, afternoon, and evening, and wrote the holy words from the Pentateuch on the wooden beams of his doorpost. If he could not convert, he would be a Jew in practice.

When Nicholas Antoine was ordained a Christian minister, he never referred to Jesus, and always quoted from the Old Testament. In his sermon one Sunday, he elaborated on his belief that God is all spirit and therefore could not have had a son. An important church official in his congregation had him promptly arrested. Brought before a tribunal, he refused to defend himself, stating simply that he was a Jew.

The tribunal pronounced him insane and incarcerated him in an asylum. In a last attempt to be Jewish, he tried to circumcise himself with a piece of ragged metal. Word of this got out, and the officials dragged him once again before the tribunal, sentencing him to strangulation and burning. As he was led through the streets in chains, people begged him to repent, but he refused.

The account of Nicholas Antoine staggered my imagination. Would I have had his fortitude, living in those times? I wasn't sure.

This story was about a Christian man, but the degree

of condemnation of conversion made me realize even more how dangerous it was for everyone involved. No wonder that Jews became wary of conversion. Even though the most severe repercussions to conversion occurred centuries ago, they must have left a psychic imprint. And the Holocaust, the most horrific of all persecutions, existed a scant fifty years ago, a reminder of that earlier time.

I realized that some of the suspicion and negativity I experienced as a convert was a residue from the past. A reflex, outside the scope of awareness. This was an idea I hadn't fully explored before, and it helped me see the issue from a more sympathetic perspective. I wasn't being singled out, after all.

Still, I couldn't avoid the fact that conversion had always been difficult. There was no golden age in history in which converts were brought lovingly into the community and granted full status. Although Christian persecution partly explained why this was so, it didn't provide a complete answer.

I had more to learn, and I knew I was not finished, but I came to a resting place within. The question was complex and would take years to answer. Meanwhile, I had located myself in the stream of converts through history, and was strengthened by their presence. They were my teachers. I could draw on their resolve: Nicholas Antoine wouldn't have been dissuaded by the insensitive remarks of the man in the print shop.

In a spirit of optimism coming from this new understanding, I made the decision in the fall of 1987 to marry Michael. We had been talking of marriage throughout our relationship, one of us wanting it, the other not, back and forth. The time in Israel had almost broken us apart. But now I was a converted Jew and on my way to gaining strength and confidence. I felt prepared to take this next step.

The wedding preparations began in earnest. This was to be the largest, most traditional of weddings. Although I had had a big wedding before, Michael had not, and he wanted one. At first I had objected, as it seemed inappropriate for me, a divorcée. But when I realized that Judaism doesn't regard divorce in the past as failure, and it considers every marriage a time of *simchah,* joy, I changed my mind.

Three weeks before the wedding, I received a call from one of the rabbis who was slated to perform our ceremony. This rabbi, who was orthodox and coming from the East Coast, had an offer to make. "When I'm there for your wedding," he said, "I'll convert you."

I was stunned. "But I'm already converted. It's been months."

"I know. But if you ever move to Israel, you'll need an orthodox conversion," he replied.

I felt my defenses rise. "Thank you, but I'm satisfied with the way I am."

"Just think about it."

I didn't promise the orthodox rabbi anything. Even though his intention had been kind, I was upset by the idea. Wasn't my conservative conversion good enough? It certainly was for me, and should be for everyone else.

Ten days later we spoke again. "Have you thought more about the orthodox conversion?" he asked.

"Not really," I answered truthfully.

"If you and Michael move to Israel, it would be very important . . ." he began.

"I doubt that will happen," I replied. "And anyhow, I already feel Jewish. I don't need anything more."

"I'm not demeaning your conservative conversion," he said. "But there are political realities."

He certainly had a point. Hadn't I wished for the legitimacy of an orthodox conversion before I converted with Rabbi Burt? Still, I didn't want to be railroaded into something that I had set my mind against. "The logistics won't work out," I said. "You won't be in town long enough."

"No problem," he replied. "We'll do it the morning of your wedding."

My resolve began to break down. The advantages of an orthodox conversion could not be denied. It might even help me feel more legitimate as a Jew, since it would be accepted within the religious community as authentic. And this rabbi, who I respected, promised to do it quickly. When else would I have such an opportunity?

I called him back two days before the wedding, telling him I would accept his offer. "That's a wise decision," he replied.

The day of the wedding arrived, a bright warm January day in 1987. The night before I had stayed at my sister's home, spending my final hours of singlehood away from Michael so that the coming together at the wedding would be all the more joyous. Early this wedding morning I rose and went to the orthodox synagogue where the *mikveh* was, the place where I had had my first conversion with Rabbi Burt.

The trip to the synagogue was different from when I had driven across town with Michael many months ago. This time there was no excitement, no anticipation. Displeased about spending my wedding morning this way, I chided myself for agreeing to the conversion. But I told myself that it was just a formality and would soon be over.

Entering the synagogue, I saw the two men who were to be the official witnesses of the conversion. These men, who I knew only slightly, were members of the orthodox shul, and they were pacing back and forth, waiting for the rabbi from the East Coast to show up.

"Are you sure your rabbi made the proper arrangements with the rabbi of this synagogue?" one of the men asked testily.

"I assume he did," I answered, not so sure.

"If he didn't, I refuse to be part of this conversion," he said.

"Me, too," the other man added.

I sank to one of the folded chairs across from them. How did I get involved in this, I asked myself.

"Who is this rabbi, anyhow?" the first man said. "Are you sure he has the right credentials?"

"Of course," I answered.

"I won't have anything to do with this if it is not above board," he replied. "It has to be done according to Jewish law."

The men glowered at me, and I could think of nothing to say that would ease the situation. I wished they would leave, but I needed them for my conversion. When I agreed to the orthodox conversion, the rabbi had told Michael and me to find two observant orthodox men to make up the Beit Din. This was the best we could do, given my relationship to the orthodox shul.

I waited silently with these men for almost an hour, until the rabbi from the East Coast finally arrived. "Did you make the arrangements?" the witnesses asked, leaping on him. "Are you sure everything is kosher? We won't participate unless it is."

"No problem," he answered. To allay their suspicions, he described at length his telephone call to the rabbi of this synagogue.

"So, we can begin," he said, when they finally settled down. "Good. Nan, do you agree to continue living a life based in *mitzvot?*" By this, he meant observing Jewish law to the fullest, including Shabbat and *kashrut.* When I said I did, he told me to go to the *mikveh* and get ready for my immersion.

Surprised and relieved that this was the extent of my interrogation, I prepared myself by showering. I sang a *niggun,* a wordless melody, over and over to myself, trying to reach a state of receptivity so that the moments ahead would have meaning. I hoped that this immersion would be a recommitment to Judaism, not a trial to be endured.

The rabbi had told me to bring a white sheet to the *mikveh* with a hole cut in the middle. This was to hide my nakedness from the view of the three men, who, according to orthodox tradition, had to see me go under water. Following the rabbi's instructions, I pulled the sheet over my head, so that it draped like a poncho around my wet body.

"Okay," I called through the door. "I'm ready."

"Get in the *mikveh,*" the rabbi called back.

I carefully walked down the three steps into the tiny *mikveh.* This time the waters were freezing cold; somebody surely had forgotten to turn on the water heater. Crouching in the water, I began to shiver. "I'm in the *mikveh,*" I yelled.

The three men came into the room and stood at the edge of the *mikveh,* towering above me. I clutched the sheet to hide myself from their gaze, locking my arms over my breasts.

The rabbi instructed me to immerse myself completely. I took a deep breath and went under the gray water. The task was not easy. The sheet billowed around me, and I grabbed at it to keep my body covered.

"Rabbi, she didn't do it right," one of the witnesses said in a loud voice as I surfaced above the water. "She brushed the *mikveh* wall with her hand."

The rabbi considered the situation, then told me to submerge myself again. This time I made sure to stay in the center of the *mikveh*.

"A piece of her hair stuck out above the water," the other witness said to the rabbi, when I came up for air. "She's supposed to go under all the way." I wiped the water from my eyes, furious. Why did they have to be so rigid?

They turned to each other, discussing what to do. "One more time," the rabbi said.

"It's not easy with the sheet," I snapped. "I'm doing the best I can." Not caring anymore if they saw my body, I went under the water again.

"Rabbi, she didn't . . ." one of the witnesses began after I burst through the water.

"Enough," the rabbi interrupted.

"But . . ."

"Enough!" The rabbi turned his attention back to me. "Now3 say the first Hebrew blessing."

I muttered it angrily, then the rabbi told me to immerse myself for the next blessing. I stayed under the water as long as I could, escaping the men above, but the feeling of spiritual rededication I had hoped for eluded me.

"Rabbi . . ." the men began, when I reemerged.

He raised his hand, commanding silence. "Now do the *Shehechiyanu*."

I stood below the men, wet sheet plastered against my

nipples. Despite my desire to remain composed, despite my hope of this being a meaningful moment, tears of humiliation slid down my face into the water. "Blessed art Thou, Lord our God, King of the Universe, who has granted us life and sustenance and permitted us to reach this day." I said the traditional conversion prayer in Hebrew, my voice fierce.

By the time I finished, the men had already turned their backs on me. I was now a Jew, in the orthodox sense. I watched as they exited through the door, talking to each other, clapping each other on the back. They had done their job, but I was left with a feeling of anger and shame.

I threw on my clothes as fast as I could and left the synagogue, not bothering to dry my hair. As I drove back to my sister's house, through the January sunlight, I was shaking with emotion. They called this a conversion? Where was the spiritual meaning, the respect for the convert? I was grateful that my other conversion with Rabbi Burt had been different.

By then it was almost noon, and I was already late for the next event of my wedding day. Ironically it was to be a trip to another *mikveh*, the Chabad *mikveh*. In traditional Judaism the bride immerses herself in a *mikveh* the day of her wedding and says a special bridal blessing. Before I decided to do the orthodox conversion, I had made arrangements for four of my friends to come to the Chabad *mikveh* with me. The plan was to say the bridal blessing and spend a few moments together with them in the water, so that I would be sent to the wedding ceremony with a feeling of their support.

After the orthodox conversion, however, I had no desire to see another *mikveh*. The one I had just left had been enough for a lifetime. But perhaps the bad experience would be softened by different waters. It was certainly worth a try.

My closest friend Barbara, who had introduced me to secular Judaism twenty years before and who had come for the wedding from the Midwest, drove with me to the Chabad *mikveh.* "How did the conversion go?" she asked. "Okay," I answered, not able to talk about it.

My other friends were waiting for us in front of the Chabad *mikveh* when we arrived. This *mikveh* was in a building all its own, and its quaint wood exterior promised a more beautiful setting than the last one. "What a morning," I said to them, still upset. But when they asked what had happened, I hardly responded. "An orthodox conversion . . . it seemed like a good idea. At least it's over." They didn't press for details, and I didn't offer any, as I wanted to get beyond the experience.

I knocked on the large wood door of the *mikveh,* and the attendant, the wife of the Chabad rabbi, opened it. At first she was reluctant to let my friends inside, as they were not orthodox. But when I promised that I would do the wedding blessing by myself in the water, under her supervision, she changed her mind. "But your friends must stay out of the water until you have finished," she added.

As I entered the *mikveh,* I was relieved that it was indeed a lovely space, with light coming through the skylight, and blue tiled floors. Once again I showered and washed my hair, preparing for immersion. The blessing with the rebbetzin went quickly. Under the water I had the feeling of cleansing myself not only of my past but of the conversion that morning. The *mikveh* ritual, in its simplicity, can be symbolically very powerful.

The rabbi's wife had to leave, and she said there was no time for my friends to come in the water. I would have agreed to this, but one of my friends began to present our case. "Let us stay, please. It's a wedding day. Some songs, some blessings. Can't we at least do that?"

The rebbetzin backed down. "Okay, but make sure everything is clean before you go." She left, giving us the key to lock up the facility.

The *mikveh* was large enough to hold us all, and the water was warm and soft. Excited that we had it to ourselves, we dipped and dived, sang and laughed, told stories, exchanged confidences. I doubt the *mikveh* walls had ever heard such tales. Giddy, we were like teenagers alone with the family car.

My friends gave me blessings, crowding around me and holding me in the water. Blessings for a good marriage. A happy and creative life. Healing from past pain. Then I gave blessings to each of them. The *mikveh* was the perfect antidote for the morning.

Before I knew it, an hour and a half had gone by. If I didn't hurry, I'd be late to the synagogue for the wedding. Rubbing glycerin cream into my water-puckered skin and drying my hair, I dressed for the third time that day.

Barbara and I drove together to the synagogue, the same one where I had the orthodox conversion that morning. Michael and I had chosen it because it was large enough for the 300 people we invited, and its kitchen was kosher. As I entered, a feeling of uneasiness came over me. I was nervous about the wedding ahead as I had never been to a large orthodox Jewish wedding before. I also felt resistant to returning to the scene of the orthodox conversion. But the healing of the second *mikveh* made it easier, and the synagogue looked different now, filling up with people I already knew. The caterers were setting up tables, the florists arranging flowers, the video camera in place.

"Mom, you finally arrived!" my daughters said, surrounding me. They were wearing matching dresses, one green, one blue, a gesture that brought tears to my eyes. I had not planned to have bridesmaids at this wedding, but they had claimed their connection to me by choosing dresses that looked like bridesmaids' dresses.

"Where did you get them?" I asked again and again, clinging to them. "Do you know how much it means to me?"

I could have climbed into a corner with them and hidden. Their presence brought comfort to a day that had already been almost too full. But I needed to dress once again, this time for the wedding, and prepare myself for the many hours ahead. As I slid the cream-colored silk wedding blouse over my head and wrapped the matching long skirt around my waist, they fussed over me.

"Is your grandmother here yet?" I asked. This was the part of the wedding that made me most anxious. All my non-Jewish relatives were coming, and I was concerned about how they would react. "Please keep an eye on them," I said to my daughters. "They might find it strange."

I was having a wedding the likes of which I could hardly fathom. I had no memories to help me picture what would ensue. For the last several weeks, I had been poring over the Jewish wedding handbooks and asking questions, trying to get the details straight.

But now it was beginning. I was escorted by Barbara and my other friends to the women's tish, a gathering of the women in a separate room. I, the bride, was seated in the center, and the women danced and sang around me, stopping one at a time to congratulate me and give me advice and encouragement. Michael was in another part of the synagogue with the men, studying Torah, arguing about its meaning, being "roasted" in the traditional male way.

The women at the women's tish escorted my mother to a chair next to me. I was pleased that she had arrived, and I reached over and squeezed her hand. This was the first time she had seen my community, and I hoped that she would appreciate its sweetness of spirit and liveliness of expression.

And my older brother, he would be in the men's tish by now. Later I would see a photograph of him and the other male members of my family at this tish wearing *kippahs,* something they had not done before.

What did my brother think? Although we had been very close as children, he had grown up to be the conservative businessman in the family, and his approval of me had greatly lessened once we were adults. Was this wedding going to alienate us further?

The women at the tish swirled around, giving me blessings, hugging me, making speeches. I wanted my mother to love this culture like I did. She smiled and was gracious, but I knew she felt uncomfortable. Later she would say that she made it through the tish by the glass of wine someone gave her.

After an hour we heard the sound of the men filing through the synagogue, singing a beautiful wedding *niggun* in strong voices, escorting Michael to me. This is one of the most dramatic, sexually charged moments of a traditional Jewish wedding, with the *hatan,* the groom, and the *kallah,* the bride, coming together. And then the *bedekken,* the veiling, when the room became hushed, and Michael lowered the veil over my face, a traditional ritual to avoid a mistaken marriage, like Ja-

cob's to Leah rather than to Rachel, the woman he
loved.

Rabbi Zalman, who had flown in for the wedding, of-
ficiated over the next part of the ceremony, the signing of
the *ketubah,* the marriage contract that Michael and I had
created. As I wrote my name in Hebrew on the ornate document, I felt proud of myself, and glad that my family was
there to witness it. They might not entirely approve, but
this was who I was: Nehama.

The wedding guests were escorted into the sanctuary.
As with all Jewish weddings, we were to be married under
the *huppah,* a canopy made from a large white prayer
shawl and decorated with flowers. My children and
Michael's son were to be the holders of the four *huppah*
poles, and they went down the aisle first. Then Michael's
parents, and my mother, and finally me. The sanctuary was
filled, and as I looked around at these mostly new friends, I
could hardly believe that I was the *kallah,* here in this
place.

The wedding under the *huppah* was longer than most,
with extra songs, readings, blessings, and a sermon by
Rabbi Zalman and another by the orthodox rabbi who had
done my conversion. My daughter swayed from lighthead-
edness at standing so long. But the intimacy was intense,
with the *huppah* above and its open sides, and Michael and
me under it, making this commitment, celebrating this love
in the presence of everyone, especially our sons and daughters.

Afterward, Zalman would make a point of telling me
that he was moved by the generosity of my children that
day. "It couldn't have been easy," he said. "Yes," I answered, pleased that he understood.

The smashing of the glass ended the wedding ceremony, and everyone yelled *"Mazel tov!"* Michael and I rushed down the aisle, past all the guests, who I had almost forgotten in the moments of intensity under the *huppah*.

Immediately we were escorted into a small room next to the sanctuary, where we would be alone for a half hour. This was our opportunity to savor the intimacy of the *huppah* a little longer before the celebration began.

The door of our little room was guarded by one of the orthodox men who had been my witness at the conversion that morning. "What is he doing here?" I whispered to Michael. But then I burst out laughing: his presence could not diminish my feeling of joy. And I was amused by the image of this big, burly man with the stern face keeping everyone away from Michael's and my tender moments of intimacy.

When we came out of the room, the community once again engulfed us. *"Mazel tov! Mazel tov!"* they called. Thus began the festivities that would last another four hours. The time would spin by with toasts and speeches, food and drink, and singing and dancing.

Never had I felt so loved, so included in this community of Jews. It did not seem to matter that I was a convert. The normal divisions of everyday life were suspended for now, and I was most importantly the *kallah*. In traditional Judaism the high spiritual state of the bride and the groom on their wedding day is believed to be a channel to and from God, and people revel in being close to them. The newlyweds' love for each other provides those around them with an experience of deeper love. Knowing this, I felt connected to these people in a way I hadn't before. I was giving them something special.

In the large dining hall my family sat at a table next to ours. Throughout the evening I kept a close eye on them, watching to see if they were enjoying themselves. "How are you doing?" I'd ask, going over to them. My desire to include them in my life was so strong that I thanked them many times for coming to the wedding.

"Time for a toast," someone called toward the end of the meal, while I was sitting with my family.

"Another?" my sister laughed.

The speaker raised his glass and made a speech, then everyone clicked their glasses together. *"L'chaim!"*

At my relatives' table we clicked glasses. *"L'chaim!"* my Greek brother-in-law said.

"L'chaim!" my nephews and nieces said.

I clicked my glass against my mother's. *"L'chaim,* Mom," I said. "That means, 'To life!'"

A Jewish wife. This is what I had become. In the months after the wedding, I discovered the economy of this arrangement. One Jew married to another puts everything in its place. A life bound by tradition and simplified by homogeneity. Or so it seemed.

Although I was still a convert, I now was more Jewish in the eyes of the community. "Congratulations on your wedding!" a Jewish neighbor said to me one day when we saw each other at the grocery store. "Welcome to the fold."

An unmarried convert is hard to understand, but one who is a wife or husband becomes less strange. This person is a member of a family unit, the DNA of Judaism. Topics of conversation exist. Husband. Wife. Children. Holidays. Will you be around for Pesach? Can you come for second-night seder? The connection to the community is made easier.

However, if the conversion is known, it is never forgotten. In any Jewish community these things are whispered. Did you know that she converted before the wedding? Have you heard that he comes from a Gentile family? Even if the convert doesn't mention it, people pass the information along.

With this comes a certain stigma. Although she is a Jewish wife, or he a Jewish husband, and although the children are Jewish, the question of authenticity exists. The community watches closely for signs of differentness, like a parent watching a teenager for the first symptoms of drug abuse.

People who converted long ago do not escape this scrutiny. "What do Jews *really* think about converts?" I asked my straight-talking friend Abigail. "We buy the line that you're Jews, but we secretly think you aren't. Even if you've been in the community for years, we see you as outsiders," she answered.

No wonder, then, that many married converts hide their non-Jewish backgrounds. Wedded into Jewish families, they can more easily slide over the past. Often, when the couple moves to another community, the conversion is so carefully concealed that nobody ever learns about it.

I met such a woman recently. Relocating to Los Angeles soon after her wedding five years ago and now the mother of a young child, she pretends that she was born Jewish. She and her husband have built their social life around their conservative congregation, and she's told no one about her background.

This woman, round and dark, her long hair in a ponytail, sat on the floor playing with her baby's toes. "My best friend doesn't even know," she said. "We call each other several times a day, and we talk about everything. Sex, money, fights with our husbands. But not this."

When I asked her why, she answered: "My friend's in my congregation. I don't want it to get out."

"Because?"

"If people knew, they'd treat me differently. I like it the way it is now. I'm just another Jewish married woman."

Yet as our conversation continued, I sensed her discomfort. "Isn't it weird to be without a past?" I asked.

She sadly nodded, and then she revealed a surprising

twist. "I think my best friend is also a convert. I'd never ask, but she mentioned something that makes me wonder."

This friend had described her high school in a way that sounded like it must have been Catholic. Not much evidence, but enough to make her suspicious. Practiced at concealment herself, she could intuit it in others.

"Why don't you speak honestly to your friend?" I said. "Take a risk. It must be so strange for both of you, converts, knowing but never discussing it." I was acting like the wise older sister, but my uneasiness was increasing by the minute. This woman was mirroring my own dishonesty.

"I can't," she replied.

I felt sad for this woman who believed she was so unsafe in the community she loved. And angry with her. How could she be so deceptive? Didn't she want to be honest in her closest relationships?

Yet could I blame her? In the months after I married, I too was deceptive. I slipped into being a Jewish wife, hiding behind my married status whenever I could, no questions asked. My desire to remain hidden was a big change from the summer before, when I yearned to have the whole world know about my conversion so that the pressure of concealment would be gone.

In my community people knew about me, so I couldn't construct my identity like the woman in southern California. But elsewhere I withheld the truth. When I went to meetings in other places, representing *Tikkun*, I pretended I had been born Jewish.

This deception was not difficult. After one weekend conference, I recorded in my journal the following snippets of conversation that had taken place in the dining hall:

> *Question: "Did you have a Jewish education as a*
> *child?"*
> *Answer: "No."*
> *Question: "Did you go to Jewish camp?"*
> *Answer: "No, but I wish I had."*
> *Question: "Did you lose any family during the Holo-*
> *caust?"*
> *Answer: "No. Everyone was in this country."*

These answers fell between truth and dishonesty. They certainly gave a false impression. The story of my life became so murky that I had trouble remembering my own experience. Worse, I could not keep straight who had heard which version. The safest way to handle this was to be as silent as possible, or at least remain cryptic about the past.

As always, I felt shabby. Not only was I misrepresenting myself, but in my deception I was disloyal to my non-Jewish relatives. If I did not claim them, wasn't I abandoning them? The guilt increased. Clearly something would have to be resolved.

In the months after the wedding, my responsibilities at the magazine solidified. With additional staff, my supervising responsibilities increased, and I spent my time devising systems to handle the heavy office flow. Never had I done work like this before. Sorting and sifting, tracking and tracing, this was hardly the creative activity I had imagined when we first began the magazine.

Frequently newspaper reporters or television crews visited us to do stories about the magazine. Lured by Michael's expert media outreach, these people found their way to our office, shaking their heads at the incongruity of a national magazine being run out of an A-frame tree house in the California hills.

"I can't believe this place," said the *Newsday* photographer, who had flown in from New York to take pictures of us. We laughingly posed for him, bent over the desk, outside on the deck, grinning, flashing copies of the magazine, proud of ourselves for what we had accomplished.

The moment was exciting, but on the whole our life was less glamorous than it appeared from the outside. Michael was on the phone from morning until evening in his office in the basement, and upstairs I managed the magazine business. We were the traditional couple, he the world-connected magazine father, and me the nurturing magazine mother.

When I asked myself if I was satisfied, I hardly knew how to answer. More than anything, I yearned for stability. After all the change and disruption of the last few years, I didn't want to do anything that would upset the balance at work or at home. If this meant ignoring my feelings of frustration and discontent, I would do it.

In those placid and hardworking months after our marriage, my identity as a Jew became more solid. It now was an internalized fact of my existence rather than a surprise every time I thought of it. After all the insecurity, this was a relief.

Sometimes it seemed that I had been Jewish all my life.

One afternoon I left work to meet a new friend at a cafe for lunch. Having just returned to the United States from sixteen years in Israel, this friend began to describe her ambivalence about being back.

"I know what you mean," I said with great feeling. "I was in Jerusalem for two summers, and there's no place like it."

"I'm surprised you feel that way," she said.

"Why not? I've had some of the best moments in my life there, and some of the worst, but I love it more than anywhere. The rocks, the trees, the sky. The feeling of history." Once started, I could have gone on and on.

My friend, who knew I was a convert, looked at me skeptically. "I understand why someone who's born Jewish feels that way, but why you?"

"I don't know," I shrugged, although secretly I considered this attachment to Israel another sign of my true Jewish nature.

After this conversation my friend would frequently remark about my unexpected connection to Judaism. "An attachment to Israel is ethnic. It's in the blood. I still don't know how you, a convert, can feel it."

"It's just who I am," I'd answer proudly.

I often marveled at how natural my Jewishness felt. Being married made a difference, but there was more. Sometimes I thought that I had been Jewish in a past life, although I hardly believed in such things. My connection to Judaism was so deep that it astonished even me. It was like coming home, as Rabbi Zalman had suggested before my conversion.

But how could an ethnicity that was unknown in childhood seem so familiar? Home is the smell of food, and the softness of the bed, the conversation around the table, and the touch of a parent. These things appear to be so unique, so specific, that they cannot be replicated.

One evening I was in the kitchen making matzoh ball soup, and I had a flashback. I remembered my mother making a similar soup. The base was much the same, a chicken, some onions, a carrot or two, and then she dropped in the dumplings, which were about the size of the matzoh balls simmering in my soup.

This memory helped me begin to connect the past with the present in a fuller way. I had already understood the relationship between converting and the creek, and I had made the association with Grandma Alice. Now I moved to a more subtle level, ferreting out the similarities between the culture of my childhood and Jewish culture.

I felt an urgency to bridge the gap between the two. I did not know it then, but the catalyst was my deception about my background. I was so appalled by my dishonesty that I was forced to find a way to reconcile my past.

Food. This was the easiest connection. Jewish Ashkenazi food reminds me of the food of my childhood. Stewed vegetables, meat cooked until it falls apart, rich deserts. My memories of food center most strongly on the Missouri ranch, a fenced-in hideaway in the Ozark Mountains where my mother's parents, Grandpa and Mummy, lived half the year. Each autumn we visited these grandparents. In the big dining hall three huge meals a day were served, prepared by the cooks according to Mummy's recipes. The food was so fattening and delicious that it is still talked about in my family today.

The honey cake I make at Rosh HaShanah reminds me of my grandmother's apple cake, and the meals I prepare for Jewish holidays are just as bounteous.

But this comparison has its complications. My grandparents' ranch in the Ozarks covered 13,000 acres. Deer, elk, buffalo, squirrel, and pheasants roamed this wild land, and hunting was one of the main activities. Every morning the men left the house early, dressed in camouflage clothing, slinging their rifles over their backs. They returned later with their bounty splayed over the hood of the truck.

Hunting is not a Jewish activity. In Judaism a reverence for all life exists, although the killing of animals is accepted as necessary because of human desire for meat. Jews don't take the death of animals lightly. Only unblemished, fully grown animals are supposed to be slain. Their throats are ritually slit under the guidance of the *shohet,* and the flesh is salted, the blood drained, so that no person has contact with animal blood. In recent years I've learned that the killing of these animals is not as humane as it should be in this age of technology, and the animals sometimes suffer more than necessary. Still, the impulse of reverence exists within the religion.

What was the connection between the hunting culture at the ranch and Judaism? They could hardly be more dissimilar, but in my desire to make my life more coherent, I sensed that one existed. The key to this mystery seemed to be my grandfather.

Grandpa grew up in the Ozark Mountains in a family of fourteen children, his father an itinerant Baptist minister. When he graduated from high school, he married his childhood sweetheart, Mummy. Together they went to Idaho to homestead, and Grandpa worked as a well-driller until he saved enough money to buy his first grocery store. One store led to another, and in this way he founded a large national chain of supermarkets. The tension-laden life of a businessman threatened to overwhelm him, however. Ill and emotionally depleted, he returned to the Ozarks and bought the ranch that we visited. Around his land he built a twenty-foot-high fence.

By the time I knew this grandfather, his life was arranged to protect him from further pressure. Sitting in his big leather armchair at the ranch and smoking a cigar, he seemed at peace. But under the surface, he was plagued by a terrible anxiety about his health and a fear of death.

Mummy, his great love, consoled him, and together they constructed a life of safety at the ranch. During their six months there each year, they ignored the rest of the world and returned to their roots. To do this, however, required a stretch of the imagination.

"We're country people," Grandpa would say, looking fondly at Mummy. "We live off the land." Even as a child, I found these remarks strange. He was the richest man I knew, his life far more comfortable than those who had to work the land to survive.

Because of my grandparents' desire to return to a simpler life, they ate only what grew at the ranch. This included animals. When Grandpa sent the men out in the morning to hunt, he was doing it for a reason. People at the ranch must be fed, and the land must be maintained by keeping the wildlife balanced.

As a child I could see the excitement in the hunters' eyes and the pleasure they felt in killing. But Grandpa's rules kept the underlying violence under control. Young deer could not be killed, nor injured deer, nor fawns, and nobody could shoot a wild elk or buffalo without permission. If a man acted irresponsibly, he would be sternly chastised by my grandfather and banned from further hunting.

The care Jews give to the killing of animals is similar to the care Grandpa gave to the slaughter of wildlife at the ranch. When it was time to harvest a buffalo, as it was called, he'd sit in his leather armchair, considering which one it would be. The herd was small, only one or two dozen, and he knew each animal. On the appointed day, the men would go out in the truck, traveling over the rough terrain until they came to where the buffalo were grazing.

Raising his rifle, Grandpa would pull the trigger, careful to hit the chosen animal so that it died instantly.

This was not a Jewish ritual slaughter. Yet Grandpa's concern for the animals and his insistence that there be no unnecessary killing gave it a kind of elevated status. I am searching here for a connection between this part of my childhood and being a Jew. It is faint, but when I first learned about kosher meat and where it came from, the process of slaughter seemed familiar. I thought of Grandpa.

At any point I can go into my life and find something that connects the past with the present. Just as I acknowledge the differences between Jewish and Gentile culture to see how far I've come, I draw upon the commonalities between them to make my life into a coherent whole. My grandfather was not a *shohet,* but he was trying to find a way to provide meat within a moral framework. The elements, although not the same, are related.

The search for continuity in my life persisted. My ancestors came to America from northern Europe in the eighteenth and nineteenth centuries. Like so many other immigrants, they settled on the East Coast, then moved west. Grandma Alice was part of that westward migration. As a small child, she traveled by covered wagon across the Great Plains and settled with her family in a small town in the northern California mountains.

My other grandparents had similar histories. Grandpa Ed's family arrived in California before his birth, although Grandpa and Mummy did not arrive until adulthood. By the time I was born, all my relatives had established themselves in California, but I knew that their days of unsettledness were not far behind.

My family's experience of moving westward rooted itself in my imagination. As a child I used to pretend I was a pioneer. I built sod houses on the prairie and crossed the Rockies and the Sierras, until finally I descended into the fertile land of California. Over and over I lived the moment of discovery of this new world. "Look!" I'd shout, "The grass, the trees, the valleys!" It would take many decades before I knew the *Shehechiyanu* prayer, but the spirit of thankfulness was the same.

I first learned about the early Jewish pioneers in what is now the country of Israel when I was twenty, pregnant with my first child. I pictured them being like my family, sustained by a dream, moving on until they finally reached their new home. Once there, they labored hard, just as my relatives had, and they survived by their effort and their intelligence.

This was an idealized version of the Jewish experience. I've read about the terrible hardships these pioneers endured, the toil to control the land, the people who died on the way, the pain of leaving loved ones behind. Still, the spirit of pressing toward a promised existence is familiar to me, and it is my heritage.

My family's experience parallels Jewish experience in another way. Like many Jews in this country, my grandfather and father became wealthy by providing items that people needed for everyday life.

My father, with his hair brushes and sewing notions, and his toothpaste and laundry soap, was like the father of a Jewish friend of mine, who started out selling buttons and ended up amassing a fortune. There is a certain feeling to people like this. Their occupation as merchant is considered lowly, but their status rises as they accumulate money and power.

As a teenager, I thought that my father was a failure.

"You're just a businessman!" I'd fling at him when he tried to convince me his opinion was right. In my mind his work contributed nothing of value to humanity. I would have liked him to be a doctor, or a teacher, or an artist.

"I give the public what they need," he'd reply in a hurt voice. "Isn't that something?"

The American dream was a reality for my family, as it has been for many American Jews. Certain characteristics are shared: The feeling of disorientation that comes from changing class and status. Stories of past poverty told to children and grandchildren who know only comfort. "Remember," it is said, "you would be poor if not for us." The possibility of destitution is always there. Mummy collected bits of string and rubber bands.

My father explained the American Dream to me: if you work hard and if you are smart, you will be successful. Even as a child, this concept did not make sense.

In our home in the suburbs my parents employed an English family that immigrated to the United States after World War II. I'd follow Bill, the gardener, around the property as he pruned plants and fertilized the lawn. He seemed to know how to do everything, a smart man. His wife Priscilla and her sister Ruth cooked and cleaned from early morning, when we came downstairs for breakfast, until evening, when the dinner dishes were washed and put away. Despite their long working hours, their lives did not seem to improve from year to year. What did this say about the American Dream?

I struggled with this, and more. Like other children who grow up in newly rich homes, I could not figure out why good fortune had come our way. Luck seemed to be involved, although I couldn't be sure.

The issue of money plagued me for decades. As a

teenager I tried to separate myself from my family's wealth. My friends wore cashmere sweaters to school but I wore only wool, and I refused to drive the family Cadillac. I'd get up early and take the school bus instead. If I was driven home by someone who had never been to my house, I asked to be dropped off a quarter-mile away, so that they wouldn't see the Louisiana plantation-style mansion with its white columns and circular driveway.

My denial of wealth continued after I left my family's home. Living in the East and then in the Midwest with my minister husband, I hardly allowed myself to think about my inheritance. In the spirit of the sixties I considered myself to be a radical, opposed to private wealth. Capitalism had done great harm, and I was ashamed of my connection to it.

Only when I reached the age of forty did I finally accept the responsibility of my inheritance. With this, I felt relief. I was no longer living a schizoid life, denying money yet benefiting from it. My inheritance had been a burden, but now it was a resource to do important work in this world. Later I would use it to start *Tikkun* magazine.

I've known many Jews who have gone through a similar shift of understanding about money. At colloquiums on socially responsible giving, the children and grandchildren of successful Jewish immigrants usually make up a sizable part of the audience. There are cultural differences: those born Jewish are more likely than I to have been trained as philanthropists by their families. But the emotional issues are the same, and in this way I feel that these people are my colleagues.

When I entered the Jewish world, I felt more at home because I knew many Jews who shared my class background and were concerned about the same issues. I am not saying that most American Jews are wealthy. Far from it. But overall, Jews have been economically successful in this country, and within the community I find others like myself.

Judaism, and the values inherent in it, helped me become clearer about my relationship to money. One of the basic tenets in the religion is *tzedakah,* righteous giving through charity. Jews take on the responsibility of caring for each other, and participate in the healing of the larger world through sharing their resources.

Money is demystified in Judaism. Instead of something that causes shame, or something that is considered dangerous, or something to be hoarded, it is a resource.

Everyone has the responsibility of giving, and those who have more wealth have added responsibility. These were values I had established for myself before I became Jewish, but they were strengthened by becoming part of a community that holds this belief.

My conversion did not end with the immersion into the *mikveh.* Afterward, I, like others, went through many stages of adjustment, each with its own peculiarities.

It seems strange in retrospect that I became obsessed during this time with food, and the Missouri ranch, and my family's experience with money. But I was putting together the disparate pieces. Slowly my history seemed less fractured, my mood less frantic. As I integrated the past into the present, I felt more secure within myself. Now I had more emotional resources to combat the disorientation I often felt as a convert in large groups of Jews.

One fall weekend I traveled to a hotel in the Catskill Mountains to attend a meeting of rabbis and Jewish leaders from around the country. As the publisher of *Tikkun,*

I had been invited to observe these proceedings, which included discussions on such issues as the future of American Judaism and the relationship between the denominations.

The content of the conference interested me, but even more, I was fascinated by the participants. Still a newcomer to organized Jewish life, I didn't know most of them. As they parried their comments back and forth, it became clear that they were bound by personal loyalties that eluded me, and they represented organizations that I could hardly keep straight. Was it American Jewish Congress or American Jewish Committee, Jewish Community Center or Jewish Community Relations Council, CLAL or CAJE? The names swam together.

I carried on my end of conversations, trying to appear relaxed and competent, but my mind was working overtime. It was all I could do to keep myself oriented. I didn't want to discredit the magazine with a silly slip of tongue, or reveal my inadequacies.

After a lengthy symposium in which the subject of Jewish solidarity had been raised, I took a breather in the hall. I had gotten lost in the argument about denominations, and I felt as if I was in a foreign land, perhaps Tibet or Senegal. What was I doing here?

But then a man slipped out of the meeting room and into the hall, lighting a cigar. We nodded at each other. The smell of his cigar reminded me of Grandpa. The man even looked like him, with his dapper jacket, his silver hair, and his frown. Already I felt better.

He was silent, and I could think of nothing to say. He must be a businessman, I decided. Moving up the ranks of Jewish leadership as a philanthropist. Perhaps his children had been in the audience with me at one of the meetings for socially responsible investors. His familiarity made me feel more composed.

At the end of the hall a waiter opened the doors to the kosher dining room, where lunch was soon to be served. I had checked the menu earlier, and knew we would have baked fish, macaroni, and green beans, with garden salad and rolls on the side and chocolate pudding for desert. This was an unexciting but familiar meal, like the food I sometimes ate as a child.

At lunch people would speak of their families, and I'd hear stories of grandparents coming to this country, children moving to Israel, lives put together and undone. And I'd listen quietly, thinking of Grandma Alice's trek across the plains to California and Grandpa's rise from poverty to wealth. The connection between my experience and theirs would be stronger than the feeling of disorientation.

The crowd began to filter out of the meeting room. I was now surrounded by people who seemed more familiar. This wasn't a foreign country, after all. It might be Canada or even England, but the language was the same and I was safe, even if I couldn't remember all the details of Jewish organizational life or everyone's affiliation. I drifted along with the crowd to the dining hall, more comfortable, more sure of myself. I was among my own kind.

I'd like to stop my story here, the convert settling into a new life. The past and the present reconciled. A promising marriage.

The outlook for the future was good, but it did not materialize. Under the surface of my marriage to Michael there were too many cracks. Some of them existed from the beginning, our woundedness, our proclivity to repeat destructive patterns. Others emerged as issues between us. In the months ahead these cracks would widen, so that the ground cover, the new life, would not take hold.

One of these cracks was anti-Semitism. Even now, I am surprised that this issue caused such personal difficulty. Anti-Semitism separates Jew and Gentile more than any other, and as such, it separated me from myself and from those I loved.

My life before I converted did not prepare me for this. The issue of anti-Semitism points out my weakest link to Judaism. Through the generations no one in my family was hurt, or killed, or discriminated against because of anti-Semitism. Quite the opposite. My family existed on the other side, part of the system, part of the web of oppression. As their child, I had a life experience different from that of those born Jewish.

I did not know about anti-Semitism when I was young. My father, who lectured about ethnicity, never talked about Jews. The colored, as he called African Americans, were inferior, and Mexicans were lazy. Chinese were clannish, and Italians were irresponsible. He stereotyped his way through the ethnic list, but Jews were not included. I've puzzled over this for years, but never understood why.

In the suburban community where we moved when I was eight, there were several Jewish families. But most Jewish students, those with the last names of Shapiro and Pinkus and Rappaport, never spoke of their religion, and only later did I realize who they were.

In my church I learned about the existence of Jews. My eighth-grade teacher told me that Jesus was a Jew, something that surprised me because I always thought of him as a Christian. But she assured me that he was a good Jew, better than the rest, the one who overturned the money tables in the temple because of the priests' corruption, and the one who led the way to a religion that was an improvement over Judaism.

"Judeo-Christian" was a concept I heard about as a teenager. It meant that Jews and Christians were two branches of the same tree. Although we were different, we shared the common base that was the foundation of Western culture. Because of this, we should regard each other with goodwill, even though Christianity was the stronger branch.

California in the forties and fifties was booming. It seemed that wherever I looked, subdivisions were being constructed to house those moving into the state. This expansion was the topic of conversation in my family. On Sundays we'd take a drive in the family car, noticing the hillsides plowed away and the new foundations being built.

"California is the most fertile place in the world," my father said. "No wonder everyone's coming here." In this atmosphere of rapid change, nothing stayed put, not even the houses that sometimes slid down the hills in the heavy spring rains.

This was a state where anything was possible. Ethnic groups mixed more in post–World War II California than in other places. Despite my father's opinions about ethnicity, the mood was one of openness. I've heard many stories of the barriers between ethnic groups on the East Coast and the curtailment of Jewish mobility during this era. But in California, we were told, life was different. Race and ethnicity did not matter.

This was a myth, of course. Ethnicity still held weight. African Americans did not live in my suburban town, and only a few Asian Americans went to my high school. If I had been Jewish, I would have another story to tell about growing up in a town mostly Christian. But I absorbed the myth of openness as part of the superiority of California, and remained complacent.

Thus I was shocked when I first heard as a teenager about the systematic murder of Jews during World War II. I search my memory to see if I had any knowledge of this at a younger age. I remember dancing wildly in a circle with my older brother when the announcement was made that World War II was finally over, but my celebration had nothing to do with saving the Jews. During the war my parents talked only about growing corn and tomatoes to feed us, and darkening our windows at night so that the Japanese would not see where to bomb if they invaded California.

I learned about the Holocaust in my high school American history class a decade later. Our teacher, Miss Rose, a dark-haired, shy woman who I now realize was Jewish, began to speak about the annihilation of the Jews. What? How could such a thing have happened? I was horrified.

Miss Rose told us we were going to see some films

about this subject in the upcoming weeks. Six hours of army propaganda films. They would be difficult to watch. Her words were an understatement. These films had been made toward the end of the war for soldiers who would soon occupy enemy territory, and the narrative was filled with invective to rile them up for the job ahead.

Hitler was the devil himself, the epitome of evil. The German soldiers were animals, crazy, and the German people degenerate followers. The images of Jews in the films were the most shocking. Stars pinned to their clothing. Shipped off in trains. Dumped into concentration camps. Starved, tortured, beaten. Hundreds and thousands of bodies in pits.

After the first film I felt as if I had been pummeled. "If you need to remain in the classroom for a while, you can," Miss Rose said. I stayed on, weeping, not even noticing if others were there.

I do not remember who I told about those films. Probably not anyone in my family, as we did not discuss such things. The conversation at the dinner table each night was limited to pleasantries spoken in turn and reminders about manners. Torture and death would not have fit in.

But I could not stop thinking about what I had seen. The question of evil dominated my consciousness. How could humans do this to each other? And what about God? I began to read books about the Nazis and the Jews, William Shirer's *Berlin Diary* and Anne Frank's *Diary of a Young Girl*. The destruction of the Jews seemed to be part of something larger, the evil of the human race.

Although I was a Christian, and living in California, I began to identify with the Jews in the film. Their suffering was far beyond anything I knew, but when I pictured myself in Europe during those war years, as I so often did, I thought without a doubt that I would be Jewish.

In retrospect, it seems presumptuous and disrespectful to the Jewish experience that I did this. I do not know even now why I felt this way. Perhaps it was the heightened emotionality of a teenager, or the painful feeling of being different from others in my suburban culture. Or a foreshadowing of the future.

This was the first breakdown of my identity as a Christian. Jewish was no longer "other," at least in this instance. I did not realize the implications of my emotional shift. Reading whatever I could find about the Jewish experience during the war, I adopted a feeling of despair about the human condition. On my treks to the City Lights bookstore in San Francisco, I'd pass by people in North Beach coffee shops who seemed to be like me, discussing philosophy and dressed in dark colors. They exuded the same cynicism. Although I didn't know it then, I was witnessing the beginning of the Beatnik movement.

When I registered as a freshman at a college in southern California, I was assigned a roommate who was Jewish. On that first day, arriving at college after the long drive south, my parents took my new roommate and me out for dinner. We were awkward in the presence of my parents, but late that night our confidence grew, and soon we were telling each other secrets and sharing photographs of our most recent loves.

"I'm Jewish," she said, just before we went to sleep.

"Oh," I answered, pleased.

A few weeks later when I called home, my father asked if I liked my new roommate. I said I did, a lot, and then proudly announced that she was Jewish.

"I knew that," he replied.

"You did?" I couldn't imagine how he had gotten such information.

"It was obvious the first time I saw her."

"What do you mean?"

"Her nose."

I began to laugh loudly, raucously, angrily. "That's impossible," I said. "Her nose is smaller than mine. She had a nose job when she was sixteen." This had been one of her late-night secrets.

"It's still obvious," he retorted.

By this time I was well seasoned in arguing with him. "You don't know anything about this," I said. "You're just stereotyping."

We never talked about the matter again. In the future I realized that he must have been aware of the large Jewish population in my roommate's hometown, Beverly Hills, and he probably recognized her last name as Jewish. Still, the nose part bothered me. Didn't the Germans think the same way?

In my Sociology 101 class that first semester, I read *The Authoritarian Personality*. Here was an important discussion about anti-Semitism. These scholars were trying to figure out why people like my father made racial stereotypes, and I was fascinated. I would major in sociology, I decided. The decision held firm, even though I transferred after three semesters to the University of California in Berkeley, and married my first husband.

Before I converted I believed that I bore responsibility for anti-Semitism. As a Christian, I could not avoid it. "The buck stops here," we sixties' radicals used to say about racism, and in my mind I extended this to anti-Semitism. Since I belonged to what we called the white Christian ruling class, I was associated with the harm done to Jews.

I often spoke out about anti-Semitism. From my reading in sociology I thought I knew enough about it to identify it in its most subtle forms. Priding myself on my understanding, I considered myself sensitive to the Jewish experience.

It is one thing to know about anti-Semitism and to take responsibility for it as a Christian, and another to become its target, however. After my conversion, my relationship to anti-Semitism went through a profound change. As I experienced it myself, rather than seeing it from the outside, I felt confused, defensive, and angry.

My first experience of anti-Semitism as a Jew took place soon after I married Michael, as I was getting ready for Passover. I had stopped by my neighborhood fish market on my way home from work to buy supplies for gefilte fish.

"I'm making gefilte fish for Passover," I told the man behind the counter. "I need white fish and pike, and anything else you can suggest."

"You're Jewish?" the man asked.

"Yes, of course."

"That can't be," he laughed. "You don't have the right kind of nose." He cupped his hand over his face, parodying a bulbous appendage.

A sick feeling arose in my stomach. Not noses again! Only this time it was directed toward me.

"You can't identify Jews that way. That's a stereotype," I said, in the same cold tone I had used with my father years before. I was incensed with this man not only for his slur on Jews but because he had the temerity to say I didn't look Jewish.

"Don't be offended," the man replied, piling fish on the scale. His tone did not sound at all remorseful.

"Lots of us have noses that are small," I continued. When he didn't answer, I let the subject drop.

As I left the store, the man smiled at me. "Have a nice day." Clearly he was not bothered by our interchange, but I was shaken.

Afterward I began to question myself. Why hadn't I stormed out of the store? I could have made more of a scene, but I was bound by long-standing, internalized rules of politeness. What did this say about my Jewish commitment?

More confusing, the man behind the counter easily could have been a relative. The name on his name tag said "George Smith," and he looked a lot like my father or my brother. He must have seen the same similarity in me, and assuming that I came from his side of the ethnic line, he took the liberty of making the comment about noses. One Christian talking to another, an insider's joke.

Had I transmitted uncertainty about my Jewish identity, thereby giving him permission? I was outraged, but it was easier to criticize myself for catalyzing this man's comments than to stay with the feeling of anger.

In those early days after my conversion, I did not want to think about anti-Semitism. I had studied it as a Christian, but now I was a Jew. My concern was finding a place for myself within the Jewish community, not monitoring the actions of those people I had left behind.

I tried to push the experience in the fish store to the back of my consciousness. When the memory returned, as it did every so often, I reminded myself that the comment about noses, although obnoxious, was nothing compared to real persecution. The guy was a jerk, period. One incident didn't mean that anti-Semitism was a major problem. After all, this was the United States, a good place for the Jews.

I knew about anti-Semitism, but it was too much for me to grasp that I, a converted Jew, was now its potential target. My WASP privilege would no longer count. Instead of realizing how vulnerable this made me feel, and how ashamed I was of this reaction, I tried to convince myself that anti-Semitism was not a serious matter.

In our household I took the position of minimizing anti-Semitism. When the subject came up around the dinner table with Michael and his son, I'd argue that the non-Jewish world was not as threatening as it sometimes seemed. I knew about it firsthand, having been Christian, and I hadn't noticed much evidence of anti-Semitism growing up. The tone in my voice was defensive, daring them to disagree.

I'd suggest that if we Jews took every glance, every remark of uneasiness by non-Jews and labeled it as anti-Semitism, we were slipping into paranoia. Rather than naming trouble, we were searching for it.

Many Gentiles in America are simply ignorant about Judaism, I went on to explain. They assume that it is just another American religious denomination, not quite Christian, but one that exists along the same continuum. Comments from these people are sometimes insensitive, but they are not meant to be malicious.

Certainly there are non-Jews who are more hostile, I allowed. These are the ones who perpetrate the ugly stereotypes of Jews that exist in the larger culture. At the far edge of this group are those who threaten and physically abuse us.

But I quickly reminded my audience to not forget that many Gentiles are our sister-fellow travelers. I used to be one of these myself, people who are attracted to and want to understand Jewish culture. Fueled by a love and respect for the Jewish people, they are our allies.

By going through this long explanation, I was trying to make some kind of peace with where I came from. "Accept me, accept me," I was saying. "My origins are not so bad." But my being the defender of non-Jews was confusing to those close to me. Where was that woman who had been so outspoken about anti-Semitism before she converted?

My denial of anti-Semitism was threatened soon thereafter. In the summer of 1987 *Tikkun* magazine began to organize a demonstration against Pope John Paul II. He was coming to San Francisco during his visit to the United States, and the city enthusiastically awaited his arrival. This was an opportunity to show our disapproval of the Vatican's refusal to recognize the state of Israel, and its refusal to cut off support of the Nazi-connected Kurt Waldheim, then president of Austria. A demonstration, with the attendant media coverage, would do the trick.

In those foggy summer days in the *Tikkun* office, the staff made telephone calls to others to join us in our protest, and we sat on the floor constructing signs and banners. The prospect of this protest frightened me. Although I had marched in many antiwar demonstrations in the sixties, this was different. Then I had felt relatively safe, because the crowd was large, but now I worried that our small group would be attacked.

My fear was not unfounded. After we held a press conference announcing our intention to protest against the pope, we began to receive threatening letters and telephone calls. When I arrived at the *Tikkun* office most mornings, the answering machine held a spate of poisonous curses and death threats.

"You dirty kikes," an anonymous caller, always male in my memory, would say in a cold voice. "You're going to die." Or, "Don't think you or your children are safe, you dirty Jews. We'll get you."

The threats were horrifying, but what could we do? We notified the police, and we became more watchful. Finally the day of the protest arrived, and we marched without serious incident, surrounded by police. The threats of violence continued for a week or more, then subsided.

We had been victims of anti-Semitism, but it was hard even then for me to fully acknowledge it. As time went by and the office settled back to normal, the experience seemed increasingly unreal. Those harassing letters and phone calls didn't represent anything more than a bunch of right-wing crazies. "There's always people like that," I said.

My denial crumbled several months later, however, when I met with my older cousin to interview him on tape about the material he had gathered on our family's history. In the middle of our conversation he began to question me about my conversion to Judaism. I started to answer, but he interrupted, describing the "money-grubbing," "unsavory," and "clannish" Jews he had met in his lifetime.

The pleasant afternoon I had anticipated turned into a hostile encounter. Afterward I played the tape over and over, listening to his slurs against Jews and my sharp intonation. I had tried to tell him he was wrong, but he would not listen. The taping session ended abruptly, and we parted without our usual warmth.

Anti-Semitism in my family? Although I had caught a glimpse of it years ago in my father's reaction to my college roommate, I hadn't heard it from anyone else. But here it was, in its fullest expression, coming from someone in the family I wouldn't have expected, brought to the surface by my conversion. Which other family members, if they were honest, had the same attitude?

I could not pass off anti-Semitism as the irrational behavior of a fringe group. It dwelled in the hearts of those I loved, and they could direct it at me, now a Jew. The layers of protection around me seemed too thin. Vulnerable, afraid, I wanted to shield myself from these people who were suddenly dangerous.

This feeling was crystalized one evening when I went out to dinner with another relative close to me, an older woman. Sitting in the restaurant, we were making small talk over wine, waiting for the food to arrive.

"See that woman over there," my relative whispered, nodding in the direction of the next table. "Isn't her hair pretty?"

"Yes," I replied, adding that I had made an appointment to have my hair cut in a similar style the following week.

"I'm glad to hear that," she said. "Then you won't have Jewish hair."

"What?" I said, shocked.

"These last few years your hair has been too long and ratty like a Jew," she replied, without a blink.

I told her in a harsh voice there was no such thing as Jewish hair. Then I struck back in the way I knew how: "I'm a Jew, whether you like it or not."

She looked at me as though I had betrayed her, then became silent. Torn between my anger and my love of her, wishing that I could wipe away her words, I felt paralyzed. I wanted to rush out the restaurant door and leave her behind, but I couldn't. She needed to be driven home, and I was too attached to her, anyhow.

What should I do with these relatives? The question plagued me in those months after my marriage. I tried to see the situation through their eyes. They most likely felt abandoned by my conversion, their hostility to Judaism heightened by their unhappiness with me.

Still, this was no excuse. A few times I wrote them chiding letters, saying that I felt hurt and angry. Nothing seemed to work. Back and forth I went between understanding and anger. After the worst moments, I vowed I wouldn't see them again until they acknowledged their feelings about Jews, but I always relented.

"Give up on them," a friend advised. "They'll never change."

"I know," I replied. But I couldn't let them go any more than they could let me go.

As time has passed, things between us have become more settled, if not resolved. I've established my separate identity, and they're used to my being Jewish. Less defensive now, I no longer look carefully for signs of anti-Semitism.

At family gatherings, we mostly avoid the subject of my Jewish life. But once in a while I take the risk of telling them more about myself, describing Shabbat or a class at the center of Jewish spirituality where I teach. I share my pleasure about being a Jew, without expecting them to approve.

And when one of them says, "That sounds interesting," as happens occasionally, I feel that I've been given a gift.

My struggle with anti-Semitism after my conversion affected not only me. It disrupted our newly married household, causing arguments and tension. As I sorted through my feelings, I was edgy, defensive about the past, and afraid of being disloyal both to my original family and to my new religion.

The mind plays strange games. In a last-ditch attempt to defend my heritage, I began to think about the concept of human nature. This had been one my father's favorite notions, used to explain a wide variety of social behavior. Why were people prejudiced? "It's only human nature," he'd say. And why were some people violent? "Everyone has that in them. It's human nature."

I had argued with him, calling this thinking deterministic, but now I wondered. My father would say that we all have the same impulses. Did that mean that any culture, given the chance, would oppress another group in the way that Christians have historically oppressed Jews?

Without realizing it, I was trying to find an explanation for anti-Semitism that was less condemning of Gentiles. If I could let them even a little off the moral hook because of human nature, I'd feel more reconciled to my background.

But I quickly discarded the idea. I only had to think of the horrors of the Holocaust to remind myself that every culture expresses dominance and rage differently. Each has ultimate responsibility for its actions.

Once again I was back on firm ground: anti-Semitism is a choice. The threatening telephone calls we received when the pope came to town did not have to happen. Those offended by our actions could have responded differently.

Still, I wondered how Jews would act under the same circumstances. If we at *Tikkun* touched a Jewish nerve like the Christian one we pricked with the pope issue, would the expression of rage against us include threats of violence? I didn't think so, but I couldn't be sure.

Soon thereafter, I had the opportunity to find out. In the spring of 1988 we at *Tikkun* decided to issue a public criticism of Israel's occupation of Gaza and the West Bank, knowing that this would infuriate large parts of the Jewish community. The intifada was in full swing, but hardly anyone in the organized American Jewish world at that time spoke out against Israeli policy. Those who did were considered disloyal, or worse.

Looking back, our plan to bring the issue to a head was grandiose. Who were we to shake up the establishment? The power of the written word cannot be underestimated, however. Michael wrote a long magazine editorial, "The Occupation: Immoral and Stupid."

"Don't you think the title is too provocative?" I laughed, when he showed it to me.

"I suppose, but it gets the point across," he answered, my partner in this surreal episode.

The response of readers to the editorial was strong. Many letters of support, and many letters demanding cancellation of subscriptions. To reach even more people we decided to send out 350,000 copies of this editorial, flooding the American Jewish world with an alternative opinion. Tucked into a direct-mail package, the editorial would arrive in time for the 1988 Passover season.

I pored over mailing lists and organized this huge project. In each direct-mail packet we placed a request to subscribe to the magazine, a return envelope, and the controversial editorial. The gallows humor around the office was that at least our position on Israel would become known, even if nobody subscribed to the magazine and we lost a huge amount of money.

The mailing went out, and we were deluged with thousands of responses. We had made the mistake of marking the return envelope postage-paid. Irate people sent us whatever they wanted at our expense. Mostly these were angry letters, often pages long, stuffed into the return envelope, or just empty envelopes. But some people affixed their return envelope to packages containing bricks, or newspapers, or cans of food, anything to run up the expense.

The telephone also began to ring continuously. Hate calls. Once again we were the object of poisonous messages. I dreaded listening to the answering machine in the mornings, and the staff became worn down by the assault of anger.

This was like the days before the pope demonstration, but with one exception. Nobody threatened to kill us or our children. We were called traitors and worse, guilt-tripped and chided, screamed at and denigrated, but I was never afraid for my safety. Even the most poisonous messages did not intimidate me.

I had become hardened by anti-Semitism, so that this onslaught of anger was bearable. Nothing could be as bad as that sick fear of violence at the hands of Christians. We were involved in a horrendous family argument, hurtful in its own right with all the yelling and screaming, but it was not a physical attack by scary outsiders. Jews were different from Christians, at least in this instance.

Still, I was disturbed by the response to the mailing. Even though the orthodox shul had shown me the shadow side of the Jewish community, I had not expected such ugliness and venom. Nor had the others on the staff. "We did the right thing, didn't we?" we asked each other.

With the number of incidents between Palestinians

and Jews increasing in Israel, the media picked up on the controversial editorial. In newspaper articles and media programs about Israel, Michael became even more the voice of the Jewish left. We had hoped this would happen, so that the public debate about Israel would include an alternative point of view about the Palestinian struggle.

Once again I retreated to the relative safety of the magazine office. I supported Michael in the battle, glad that I wasn't on the front line, but all the more conflicted about my role at the magazine.

As the weeks passed and the criticism of the magazine continued, I tried to put my disillusionment behind me about what I was witnessing in the Jewish community. But I was expecting too much.

The tension within me needed to be aired in honest speech. At home I increasingly felt under pressure to show that I was a loyal Jew. Even though Michael and I were compatriots in the struggle to bring peace to the Mideast, we had difficulty with the subject of personal loyalty. When I revealed my negative feelings and my confusion about the Jewish community, it too often led to misunderstandings. Thus I began to withdraw into silence, a mistake because it added to the distance that was beginning to grow between us.

Soon after I married Michael, my college-graduate daughter moved into the basement of our house. Setting up an apartment, she led a separate life, and I'd see her most often at the *Tikkun* office, where she edited manuscripts.

The house was now Jewish with a non-Jewish appendage. Upstairs we'd be singing songs at the Shabbat table, and she'd be cooking dinner on the hot plate below. Her presence pleased me, but I worried that the distance between us was far greater than the sixteen steps that separated our living quarters.

When my son came to visit, this feeling was just as pronounced. He stayed in the Jewish part of the house, eating meals with us. Although he said the Hebrew blessing over the bread, and this made me dream that he, too, might convert someday, the gulf between Jew and non-Jew remained in our household. I yearned to heal it, but I could not do it by myself.

One day a conversation took place between some of my stepson's Jewish friends around the dining room table about the upcoming observance at their high school of Yom HaShoah, Holocaust Memorial Day. "Those *goyim*, they think their suffering is comparable to ours," one of the boys said. He was angry because some of the Gentile students on the organizing committee wanted the observance to include other persecuted ethnic groups such as the Cambodians.

The conversation built up steam, with the boys accusing the non-Jewish kids of everything from gross stupidity to murderous intentions, then generalizing these qualities to all Gentiles. "Wait a minute," I said, glad that neither of my children was around to hear this talk. "You're dumping too much on people who aren't Jewish."

Everyone at the table turned to look at me, the traitor. "I understand why you think that the event at your school should be only for the Jewish Holocaust, but you can't blame others for wanting their suffering to be included," I said. "You don't have to go along with them, but at least respect their feelings."

The conversation stopped immediately. Clearly I had passed over the line of acceptability. Rising from the table, I could hardly keep my anger down. What chauvinism! Didn't these teenagers understand that others were as good as they? My feelings of defensiveness about my own children, and my allegiance to them, made me want to fight on the side of the non-Jewish students, even though I agreed that the observance of Yom HaShoah should be in memory of the Jews.

Afterward I tried to calm myself. The conversation had been only an exercise of youthful passion, something that ordinarily amused me. These kids were *mensches,* and they were welcome in my home. But try as I might, I couldn't get beyond my anger.

Through this and other experiences in my personal life, I began to identify the existence of Jewish chauvinism. At its roots was the question of whether Jews are better than others. Too often, the answer seemed to be yes.

Outside our home I was often privy to conversations about Gentiles, the kind that take place in a room of Jews when no one else is around. Now that I was a Jewish wife, my background was temporarily forgotten, and people were more likely to express what was on their minds.

These conversations usually began with someone re-counting an incident that involved a Gentile. At first the in-sinuations of stupidity, or insensitivity, or cultural obtuseness were veiled, but then the description became more direct. Sometimes they'd reach the level of "*Oy*, the *goyim*," accom-panied by snickers.

And always I would think: my children, my children.

I didn't speak out against this talk. It was one thing to reveal myself to the teenagers who often hung around our house, and another to do it with people I hardly knew. I didn't have the courage. Besides, I didn't want to draw at-tention to my convert status. I was even flattered that these people trusted me enough to reveal their feelings in my presence. But my internal conflict was so great, and the depth of their disregard so strong, that I could not laugh and carry on the conversation afterward.

From my professional training I knew that this dispar-agement of non-Jews came at least partly from past oppres-sion that led to a feeling of inferiority. It was self-hatred, turned on its head. But that wasn't all of it. Many Jews, in fact, seemed to carry feelings of superiority, alongside whatever negative self-images they might have internalized. As one of my friends said to me, "Jews are best. It comes down to that."

But don't all people think this about themselves? Probably so, I decided. I had grown up with my father telling me that our ethnic group was superior. "People who come from the northern climates are the best stock," he'd lecture. "They're the most intelligent, the most industri-ous." Translated, this meant that white Protestants were at the top of the heap, something he hardly needed to say as it was assumed in the culture around me.

From an early age I had argued with my father about this attitude, saying that all people are fundamentally the same. Now that I was Jewish, however, the issue of ethnic worth became far more complicated.

Did I have the right to criticize other Jews for their statements of superiority? It was one thing to fight with my father about this issue, but another to fight with these people whose life experience had been different from mine. Although I was now a Jew, I was afraid my criticism might sound anti-Semitic.

I began to question why I was so charged about this issue. Perhaps my pride was wounded by my children being assigned to the "inferior" side of the equation by Jews. Or maybe I was having trouble giving up the Christian privilege that I had known all my life. Or was it just too painful for me to acknowledge the negative aspects of the non-Jewish world?

My confusion deepened. One autumn day I was invited to give a lecture about Judaism in a nearby retirement community. This was an assignment I welcomed, an opportunity to be the expert about my newly embraced religion.

"In Judaism the concept of chosenness exists," I found myself saying toward the end of my talk. "Jews have a special relationship with God, based upon our experience at Mt. Sinai."

I thought nothing more about this, but afterward a small man in a pale blue jogging outfit approached me. "Your speech was good," he whispered, "but you shouldn't have spoken about us being the chosen people. These folks might take offense."

I followed his glance around the room, where the audience was sipping coffee in groups of twos and threes.

"Most of these people are Christian, and you have to be careful," he said. "Believe me, I've lived longer than you."

Thanking him for his advice, I left, but his words stayed with me. How easily I had spouted off the idea of Jews as the chosen people in my lecture. I had done it without thought, repeating something I only half understood, feeling proud as I said it that I belonged to this special group.

For the Jewish man in the audience, the mention of chosenness made him anxious. But for me, it raised an important question. By talking about chosenness, was I reinforcing the very attitude that was upsetting me so much these days? It seemed possible that I was unwittingly promulgating a belief that was at the heart of Jewish chauvinism toward non-Jews.

Jews as the chosen people. What was this historical understanding, and how did I feel about it? In my state of confusion, this seemed to be a good place to start.

I remembered back to the orthodox shul. When the Torah was read about God's revelation on Mt. Sinai, and the covenant made between God and the Jews, the people sitting around me seemed to have no doubt that this event had taken place just as it was described. The 600,000 men at Sinai, and their families and their descendents, were the chosen people. Whoever wasn't there was not included.

The people at the shul seemed certain that God had chosen the Jews over all the people of the earth. This honor brought obligations and responsibilities, to be sure, but it put Jews on a different plane, singling them out from everyone else.

Did I agree with this understanding? I wasn't sure. But I knew that every time I carefully read the account of Mt. Sinai in the *Chumash,* the Bible, I had a strong reaction. I immediately imagined myself at the foot of the mountain with everyone else. I was one of those people, witnessing the shaking and quaking, hearing the voice of God. The dry, dusty earth threatened to split open beneath me and swallow me up, and a feeling of panic arose, mixed with wonder and awe at this unbelievable revelation.

But then, I was a convert, living in the twentieth century. My ancestors were not present at Mt. Sinai. Other experiences were encoded in my DNA, not this. In my search through the family tree, not a single Semitic name popped out, not a single story sounded like the veiled tale of a Jew.

When I read in the Torah about the Mt. Sinai experience, I existed both inside and outside of it. Emotionally I felt that I belonged there, but by historical account, I didn't. I had visions of participating, although I didn't feel right claiming the experience as my own.

I had studied enough by then to know that interpretations of what happened on Mt. Sinai differ. Orthodox Jews believe that the word of God was revealed on the mountain, while the more liberal branches of Judaism are not so sure. The historical accuracy of the account is questioned by many.

However, almost all Jews I knew assumed that Mt. Sinai was a Jewish event. It was the pinnacle moment, God's revelation to the people, the big adoption. And every year the story is recounted and discussed among Jews around the world in an attempt to grasp its meaning. Past, present, and future disappear, so that Mt. Sinai becomes an experience outside of time as its revelation is explored. Although I could be part of this discussion, in reality my connection to the event was tenuous.

* * *

As a child, I staked the ground of my identity on fighting against chauvinism. I conducted this fight in the way I knew how, by claiming the moral high ground. The most permissible arguments in my family were moral. If I believed that right was on my side, I could more easily express my anger.

My father made statements with authority about the worth of ethnic groups. When I recently visited the Holocaust Memorial Museum in Washington, D.C., I came across a display of books on racial theory that fueled the Nazi movement. "Jews are racially inferior," reads one text, and then it describes the measurements of Jewish body parts, considered to be "scientific evidence" of this inferiority. My father used this same language, this same reference to science, when he described other ethnic groups. As a university student in the thirties, he must have been exposed to these ideas, since the intellectual climate that bred Nazism didn't stop at the German border.

I claimed my territory in the family at an early age. One of my tasks was to prove my father wrong. However, try as I did to change his chauvinistic attitude, I never succeeded. My father had been well schooled in his way of thinking.

I first discovered this when I was seven, on one of my family's visits to Grandma Alice's and Grandpa Ed's home in Covelo. This tiny town of 200 people was located in Round Valley, high in the northern California Humbolt mountain range. With its fields of wildflowers and its freshwater streams, this valley was the most beautiful place I knew. But to my sorrow, it held a shocking secret.

One summer evening, as we were driving on the dirt road around the valley as we usually did after dinner, Grandma Alice pointed out some charred ruins. "That's where the Indians' schoolhouse used to be," she said. Indians? I had never heard about them before.

"Why did they have a separate school?" I asked.

"They're an inferior race," she answered. "They're drunken savages. They burned down their school. Nobody's rebuilding it, because they'll just burn it down again." What had happened to my Christian grandmother, who usually preached love and justice? And why didn't my father defend these Indians? I asked a lot of questions, but they did not answer.

I finally figured out that Round Valley was an Indian reservation. When we visited Covelo in the following years, I'd see the little lean-to shacks outside of town, the yards filled with scraps of old machinery. Sometimes I'd pass one or two of the men lingering around the Covelo general store or the gas station. Unsettled by their presence, I tried not to stare.

I sensed there were things I wasn't being told about the reservation. "Indians aren't worth the time or money," my grandmother said angrily. My father agreed.

The last time I saw Grandma Alice before her death at eighty-nine, she and Uncle Jim, her brother, were arguing as they had for decades about this subject. I was leaving to go back to the Bay Area, but she was too involved in their fight to notice.

"You're wrong about the Indians!" she yelled. "They're evil, shiftless heathens!" Dust rose around her as she stamped her feet in the dirt road separating her house from Uncle Jim's.

"They're no worse than you or me," he answered, a half-smile on his face. "They're people, too."

"Goodbye, Grandma," I called, but she didn't turn around. Shouting again at Uncle Jim, she flung her fists in the air, a gesture that signified she would go on and on. "Goodbye," I whispered.

Only later did I learn the true story about these Native American people. At a Jewish renewal Yom Kippur service a few years ago, a poem, "History Lesson" by Janice Gould, was read as part of the Martyrology in the afternoon. I long ago had stopped wondering about Covelo and the reservation, but I drew to full attention when the poem began. Round Valley. Indians. Death. The words stung me.

I later verified the information in this poem. In the middle of the nineteenth century, hundreds of Native Americans were rounded up in California and driven like cattle across the mountains to the Round Valley reservation. More than half of them died along the way, shot while trying to escape. This was a tragedy of enormous proportions, one that marks them still. Since they've lived in Round Valley, their lives have been plagued by poverty, ill health, and depression.

It took over forty years for me to learn the full truth about Round Valley. Grandma Alice must have been aware of it most of her life. How could she have rationalized this tragedy? As I asked myself this question, however, I heard her voice in my mind explaining that the Indians were non-Christian and thereby inferior. They deserved what had been done to them.

When I decided to convert, I thought I was leaving behind the ethnic chauvinism of my father and grandmother. In my mind Jews were the object of anti-Semitism, not the perpetuators of prejudice. By joining the underdog, I would be free of something that had been abhorrent to me for years.

My expectations were unrealistic. Purity does not exist among any people. In the years since then, I've witnessed the Jewish oppression of the Palestinians, homes burned, detention without trial, death. And I've heard Jewish slams, slurs, and insinuations against Gentiles that are as racist as anything I heard growing up.

Still, Christian history is rife with violence toward others, and Jewish history is not. This is not to say that violence doesn't exist among Jews; certainly the suppression of the intifada, the assassination of Prime Minister Rabin, and the continuing treatment of the Palestinians prove this point. But violence is always a shock among this people, and I respect that.

The value of being respectful of all peoples is at the heart of Judaism. In thirty-six places in the Torah, Jews are mandated to treat the stranger with kindness, "for you were once strangers in the land of Egypt." This concern is also infused throughout Jewish law. For example, *lashon hara,* the law of not gossiping or passing on hurtful information, is meant to apply to relationships with Gentiles, as well as to Jews.

When I converted, I was not prepared for the complexity of Jewish chauvinism. I did not understand all the contradictions. Although Jewish law legislates against chauvinism, it seems to be encouraged, in a sense, by the belief of chosenness. And although Jews have a strong record of involvement with human rights issues, they have a legacy of distrust toward non-Jews that sometimes results in chauvinistic behavior.

Again and again in those early months of my marriage, I heard comments that astounded me with their insensitivity. Trying to understand, I returned to the question of Mt. Sinai and the concept of the chosen people. What did it mean?

A chance comment of Michael's helped me realize I was thinking about Mt. Sinai in a way that was too literal. "Have you ever been to Mt. Sinai?" I asked late one night as I was flipping through a book of photographs of the Israeli desert.

He laughed. "It's not the easiest place to find. There's a big debate about where it's located, or if it even exists."

I was astounded. The central event in Jewish history, and its geographical location was fuzzy? Somehow I had not grasped that Sinai must be a metaphor or a symbol, rather than a fact.

I had been making a cause-and-effect connection between chosenness and chauvinism. In my mind, the Jews' experience of being chosen by God at Mt. Sinai gave rise to the chauvinism that was troubling me so much. But now, if I didn't take the story literally, the possibilities expanded.

I began to search out other interpretations of the Mt. Sinai experience in the *midrashim,* the poetic interpretations of the Torah. One *midrash* says that God went to the other peoples of the world before the Jews, asking them to be partners with him. When they refused, God asked the Jews to take on this responsibility. They agreed. The author adds that the Jews' chosenness came from their commitment, not their merit. Gentiles were also worthy of this honor, even if they didn't accept it. This story softens the hard edges of being chosen, although it still confers a higher status on the Jews.

The concept of chosenness began to open up in my mind. Why not think of it as specialness? Just as each of my children is special to me, so we can say that the Jews have a special relationship with the divine. It is unique, as are all relationships, and it is our own, but it does not mean that other peoples don't have equally significant relationships.

The language we Jews use for our special relationship is the Mt. Sinai story, replete with the voice of God and the clouds of smoke. It is the moment of greatest contact of this people with the divine, and the images reveal this. What really happened? Nobody knows, but we acknowledge the intensity of the experience and the importance of the connection.

I now saw chosenness as separate from chauvinism. This made it seem possible to explore the mystery of Mt. Sinai and cherish the feeling of specialness as a Jew without reverting to chauvinism. The gap in my mind between the universal and the particular became bridged, as I recognized a way to be both a member of humanity and a Jew.

But if Jewish chauvinism doesn't come from Mt. Sinai, where does it originate? As I puzzled over this, the answer soon became apparent. With individual Jews, it seemed. Some Jews act in bigoted and prejudiced ways. This is not human nature, as my father thought, but a choice that people make.

And like other people, Jews sometimes try to rationalize their behavior. Anyone can find support for chauvinism in the Torah. On the most literal level, the drama of the "good guys" versus the "bad guys" leads to it. But the Torah's meaning is forever open to interpretation, and one can find just as many interpretations against chauvinism. The responsibility returns ultimately to each of us.

As I acknowledged chauvinism first in myself and then in others, I felt less charged about the issue. Why had I expected Jews to be different from others, anyhow? Perhaps it had been naivete, or blindness, or my dream of finding the perfect people, or even a form of condescension. But now that I saw Jewish chauvinism for what it was, I felt clearer in naming my discomfort with it.

Thus began the next stage, when speaking out about this issue became a greater possibility. As a convert and the publisher of a national magazine, I was in the perfect position to do it. If I found the courage, I could use my position to help fight against what I felt was a debilitating, destructive chauvinism. This would be done in a spirit of love, as well as with the clarity that comes from anger.

However, before I was ready, I needed to resolve my ambivalence about revealing that I was a convert. I couldn't both speak out and hide who I was at the same time. Ironically, the Mt. Sinai story helped me with this, too. As I was gathering material about the subject of chosenness, considering its meaning, I came across some interpretations of Mt. Sinai that shed light on my relationship as a convert to this event.

One *midrash* says that at the time of the Mt. Sinai revelation, the sound of the Hebrew letter *aleph,* which ordinarily has no sound, went around the world. It was felt by Gentiles everywhere who were open to hearing it and who wanted to receive it. This was a different connection to the divine revelation, but as profound in its own way as the experience of physically being there.

And another interpretation, this one attributed to Rabbi Shlomo Carlebach: At the time of the revelation on Mt. Sinai, some Jews were there who would rather have been elsewhere. These are the souls that have fallen away from Judaism through the centuries. But there were other souls that yearned to be there and couldn't. These are the ones that have come into Judaism through the centuries as converts.

Yes, I thought, when I heard these two interpretations. Mt. Sinai is much larger than the collection of people who happened to be present at the time. There was room for me, too. Whether I had a soul that resonated with the word from the mountain, or one that took many centuries to find its way there, it didn't matter. I belonged to the Jewish people on the deepest of levels, even at Mt. Sinai.

Painfully, shyly, I began to discover my public voice on the subject of chauvinism. The process was not linear or orderly. Much of the time I sensed that something was emerging, but I didn't know what.

I wanted to speak, but I was afraid. My heart beat wildly whenever I had the impulse to present my case in a public place. The stumbling block was more than being a convert. I had to get past my fear from childhood about acting in the public arena. In my family, speaking out was equated with having a bad moral character. One of the favorite sayings was, "Fools' names and fools' faces are always seen in public places." Those who managed to get their names in the newspaper were suspected of unbridled egotism and untrustworthiness.

But I was learning that change is catalyzed by action in the public arena. The uproar we caused with the *Tikkun* editorial about the Israeli occupation helped me grasp the impact of one or two voices. On a trip to Washington, D.C., when Michael and I met members of Congress who were readers, we were told that the ideas in the magazine made them rethink important issues. *Tikkun* had done this? It seemed amazing, but there it was. If we had stayed within the private sphere, it wouldn't have happened.

With all the unevenness that accompanies personal

change, I surprised myself one afternoon by speaking out against chauvinism in public. I was at an East Coast conference, in a crowded hotel room with a hundred other Jewish feminists. For the past two hours we had been grappling with issues about women's writing and publication, and the discussion had become increasingly self-revealing.

A woman in the back of the room rose to speak. I recognized her immediately as a writer and a teacher, someone I respected. "My problem is that I let myself get intimidated by Jewish men," she said. "They're so smart and articulate."

Many heads in the room nodded. "It isn't a male–female thing," she continued. "I have perfect confidence in my work with non-Jewish men." Pause. "But then, of course, you know how the *goyim* are. They're not much competition."

The room rocked with laughter, but I did not join in. The sick feeling in my belly was familiar. If she and these other women thought that non-Jews were intellectually inferior, what did they think about me, a woman who came from this background?

For a few moments I froze. A woman near me jumped up and began to respond: "I get the speaker's point, but I wish she wouldn't rely on such stereotypes. Jewish men aren't always articulate, and non-Jews aren't necessarily more stupid."

Encouraged by her boldness, I was on my feet before she even finished. "I agree," I said, my voice loud and strong. "We need to get beyond this kind of thinking if we're going to have a less chauvinistic Judaism. Some of you might not know it, but I'm a convert. It gives me pain to hear comments like that. My children aren't Jewish, nor are many others I love, but they're as smart as anyone.

Stereotypes do great harm, because they're so disrespect-ful!" There, I had said it.

My words had been a long time coming. I sat down and watched as commotion broke throughout the room. The moderator of the discussion tried to gain control: "Okay, please, let's talk one at a time. I know it's a hot topic. . . . "

To my surprise, it seemed that almost everyone agreed about the destructiveness of chauvinism. The woman who started the conversation had the last word. "I apologize," she said. "I mouthed a stereotype without thinking. This is a teaching for me."

"If we, as Jewish feminists, can't become less chauvin-istic, then who can?" the moderator said in closing. Amen, I voiced. It seemed fitting that this roomful of women was the place in which I had finally found the courage to reveal another layer of myself.

Once I found my public voice about Jewish chauvinism, other changes followed. All pretense about my background slid away. I began to speak and write about my experience, using the magazine as a forum. Soon I was known nationally as a convert. My fear of rejection didn't go away entirely, but it was pushed aside by my satisfaction at finally being authentic.

At conferences and meetings, people often approached me, sharing their conversion stories. An underground connection exists between converts; although we seldom confide, we give each other support and sympathetic glances. Many converts felt safe talking to me, but often their first words were, "Please keep this secret. Nobody knows. . . ."

At the magazine my role as the behind-the-scenes business manager had become increasingly frustrating. I had little time for my own creative work. Now that I better understood the Jewish and political worlds, I wanted to take a more active role in leadership. But speaking out was a complicated matter in the magazine setting, at least partly because I was a woman.

In 1987 a small group of remarkable, well-known writers began to meet frequently to brainstorm about future articles and ideas for *Tikkun*. Michael organized this group because he felt unsure of himself and wanted support in choosing the articles. The intellectualism of our readership was enough to intimidate even him in those earliest days of the magazine.

As publisher, I often sat in on these meetings. This editorial board was all male except for me, and on a few occasions, another woman. At each meeting we reviewed articles, ideas, and themes that had been introduced into the magazine.

My leftist intellectual colleagues had a certain style: articulate, insightful, and above all, rational. They made one brilliant and fascinating speech after another, yet the words weighed me down. There were so many of them.

I was the most silent member. I'd still be thinking about the first point, going deeper and deeper, while they jumped on to the next. After a while, I felt weary from trying to keep up.

In this setting I began to think about the difference between men's and women's thinking. Most women I knew wouldn't converse in this way, at least when they were alone with each other. There'd be more reference to relationships, more support of each other's point of view, less speech-making, less jostling and competition. Understanding the context of an issue would be more important than the final analysis.

Sitting in these meetings, my frustration mounted. This was my magazine, and I had created it with Michael, but my presence seemed to make little impact. When I threw out an opinion or a suggestion, it was greeted with a respectful, "Uh, huh," and then the conversation would go on around me.

Tikkun was an intellectual magazine. I had agreed with this concept when we started it, but now I felt disenfranchised from the process. "Face it, you're not really an intellectual," someone very close to me said, when I voiced my feelings one evening after an editorial board meeting. "That's not who you are."

Not an intellectual? I was cut to the quick by the suggestion. Had I given birth to a magazine that was so far from myself? "You're wrong," I argued. "I'm as much an intellectual as anyone, but I express myself differently."

I worried that I was less smart than the others, that the only reason I was in their company was because of the circumstance of me being the magazine publisher. In my mind intelligence became conflated with leftist male intellectualism, and I feared I didn't really have much of value to contribute.

Despite these feelings of insecurity, however, I could see that my sexual identity gave me a certain power. As the only woman, I was considered the expert about feminism and women's issues. Whenever a subject arose that had anything to do with women, the men would turn to me: "What do you think? Are we framing it right?" Seeing how frightened they were of appearing offensive, I'd take my time answering.

I also had influence as the magazine's publisher, although this was less clear. Soon after Michael and I began the magazine, we devised an arrangement whereby he held major editorial control over its contents. Money decisions were made mostly by me.

On paper I seemed to have my fair share of power, but in reality I sometimes felt that I didn't. Invested in pleasing, I often went along with Michael's abundant store of creative ideas rather than cause difficulties. This created a smoother working relationship, but at times I felt uneasy and ashamed of my lack of courage.

The editorial board members didn't know these details. In their eyes I was the one who was in charge of the business of publishing. If I strongly opposed an article or theme, I used this to my advantage. "As publisher,

I'm against it," I said. "It's not good for the magazine."

After a few rounds of trying to change my mind, the men usually dropped the idea. In the future my objections might be overridden, but at least I had the satisfaction of fending off the immediate possibility.

I was experiencing firsthand the dynamics of gender in the leftist world. In my days of activism in the antiwar movement of the sixties, I hadn't challenged the assumption that men knew more and were better leaders. But now, finally, I opened my eyes and saw this arrangement of power for what it was.

I couldn't figure out what to do. Women often use each other to check reality, but I had no one to consult. I hadn't made the connections, and I also felt embarrassed to acknowledge that I was in this situation. I should have known better.

The key seemed to be to get more women involved in the magazine so that I wasn't alone in trying to make the magazine more inclusive of women's experience. But I was up against my own failure of will and the nature of the magazine.

"I want more women writers in the magazine," I insisted at one meeting.

"We'd like that, too," replied the board. "But show us the women who can write our kind of articles." They didn't need to say more, because I knew that the tone of the magazine discouraged women writers. It was designed to compete in a national discourse that was traditionally male, rational, and intellectual, and many women felt uncomfortable with this approach.

By this time the office was receiving several hundred unsolicited manuscripts a month. We stacked them on the tables, on the floor, on the kitchen counter, wherever we found room. I scoured these stacks to find articles from women that fit the magazine, but with little success. Most of the women's articles were organized around their personal experience or written in a journalistic tone, styles we seldom included at that time, although later, after I left, these guidelines would become more flexible.

As I searched for articles, I questioned the intellectual focus of the magazine. A dichotomy had been created, with personal experience on one side and intellectual discourse on the other. This seemed artificial to me, as the life of the mind is so deeply affected by the context of experience, and vice versa.

As publisher, however, I felt I must continue to support the guidelines for publication. We had started the magazine with the goal of it having national impact. If we deviated too much from the style and content of magazines like *The New Republic, Commentary,* and *The Nation,* I feared we would be marginalized or dismissed, as our politics were already suspect.

But I was losing heart. It seemed ironic that I was finding my own voice, but women's voices were heard less frequently than men's in the magazine. It didn't matter to me that *Tikkun* was doing better than other magazines of our kind; there still weren't enough women in our pages to suit me. Without planning it, I had ended up in a world where the players were mostly male, and women existed on the fringes.

How had I gotten myself into this predicament? I was befuddled. One afternoon I took a long walk up the hill behind the *Tikkun* office. An old oak tree caught my eye, reminding me of the tree that grew outside the bedroom window of my childhood home. Thinking of the past, I began to realize that there must be a connection between my state of being and my early experience as a child. The thought comforted me: the details of this connection were unclear, but at least I had the hope of future understanding.

Some time later, after I left the magazine, I was able to see the larger picture. My relationship with my father had primed me for this painful state. Loving him as a young child, I had known that he would disapprove if I got too close to anyone else. As the center of my childhood world, he was the most important parent. I depended on him. Had I aligned myself with my mother, I would have lost him.

In the daunting atmosphere of the magazine, I repeated this scenario. Let the men lead the conversation and set the tone; let me feel diminished in the process: at least I would be loved. And in return, I would stay with them, choose them over women, give them my loyalty.

We were well-meaning people, after all. As the first generation of this second wave of feminism, we were doing our best to grapple with our fears and our inadequacies. In theory we believed that relationships should not be bound by restrictions of gender, and that we should be our most developed, nuanced selves, male and female combined. But I had been raised to care for men, and the men around me had been raised to receive this attention. These expectations shaped everything we did.

As I witnessed the men struggle with feminism, hearing both their admiration and their negativity, I could not help but feel resentful. But my anger was not only at them. Unresolved about my own role, I sank into self-criticism for not accomplishing more as a woman. As much as I tried, I could not get out of this noxious state.

My tension over this issue made its way into the intimacy of my marriage to Michael. Although it was not the final cause of the breakup, it exacerbated the difficulties between us. Sometimes I felt so overwhelmed by my frustration as a woman that I could do nothing but flee, piling a few things in my car and escaping to a place, any place, where I could be alone to regain my equilibrium. When I returned to our normal life of work on the magazine, I apologized for the disruption, vowing to myself to handle my feelings in a more reasonable way.

Michael and I could not talk about these difficulties. The subject was too painful, and attempts to communicate ended in frustration for both of us. Yet the damage increased as the months wore on.

"Perhaps we shouldn't work together," he ventured, after one more argument. "It's an impossible situation for a married couple." Yet I was reluctant to give up the partnership we had created. And like parents, we were equally committed to the magazine, our offspring.

In the midst of this, in the spring of 1988, Michael and I decided to go to Jerusalem for Passover, a time when the air smells sweet and a pale yellow light fills the city. On the first evening of the holiday we walked together along the winding streets, past blooming gardens, to a nearby orthodox synagogue for services. Just as we arrived, the eerie sound of the siren filled the air, bringing in the beginning of this holy season.

At the entrance to the synagogue I said goodbye to Michael and climbed the narrow staircase to the second floor where the women were sequestered. I hadn't been in an orthodox synagogue for some time, and the women's balcony was a shock. In California the women at the orthodox shul sat in chairs on one side of the room, across from the men, and they had no difficulty viewing the service. But here the women were put in the balcony, behind a *mehitzah* so high that the ceiling was the only visible part of the building. This barrier, made from ropes of hemp tied tightly together, was the most formidable I had seen.

Immediately my good mood evaporated. Why had I agreed to come here? My unresolved feelings about being a woman in my leftist community surfaced and merged with my anger about the way these women were treated. This anger faded into sadness, however, as I began to notice tiny holes in the *mehitzah,* slits no larger than coins on their sides. Women at past services must have made them, carefully prying these ropes apart. I squinted through one of these holes, catching sight of a few men's heads. It was useless, and I began to weep.

Why did women have to struggle so hard? In that balcony the scab of past experiences with orthodoxy was scraped open again. Only this time I had less hope: even if I never returned to this synagogue, I had my own balcony, my own *mehitzah* back at the magazine.

Afterward, when I joined Michael downstairs and we headed toward the first-night seder at a friend's home, I wanted only to be quiet. But he was ready for an evening of stimulating conversation and singing, buoyed by the pleasure of praying at the synagogue. The gulf between us widened.

I had nowhere to go with my feelings of discontent, and they seeped into other parts of my life. In Jerusalem at that time the newspapers were filled with stories of the struggle with the Palestinians. The intifada was in full swing, although most people in North America did not call it by that name. Stoning had become the Palestinians' resistance of choice, and the Israeli army was reacting harshly.

The next morning, sitting alone at the breakfast table

at our hotel, I read in the morning newspaper that two Palestinians had been killed and five wounded in the last twenty-four hours.

"My God!" I said loudly. Everyone in the hotel dining room continued to eat calmly, no one looking up. Was I alone in my horror?

A dark haze settled around me. The issue of women merged with my distress about the intifada, and in this state of mind it seemed that men were responsible for everything wrong in this world. They were the ones who sought and maintained control, and they were the ones who perpetuated violence and war. I felt I was finally acknowledging a truth I had previously resisted.

The story of Passover is central to Jewish belief and understanding. When I first heard it, in my twenties at a Passover seder, I resonated with its theme of freedom from bondage. The Jews were once slaves in the land of Egypt, the story begins. After God brought many plagues against the Egyptians, Pharoah released the Jews. They fled to the Red Sea, Moses leading the way, the Egyptians in pursuit. It seemed that they would be slaughtered, but the waters of the sea miraculously parted and they passed safely through to the other side.

Every year Jews remember this experience of slavery and freedom by celebrating Passover. Gathered together in their homes for the seder, a ritual dinner that goes late into the night, they discuss the meaning of this pivotal event in Jewish history.

Every year in my memory, someone at the seder table makes the analogy between crossing the Red Sea and birth. The passageway out of slavery was narrow and constricted, like the birth canal, and the process difficult, yet it led to a life of freedom. People speak about their own personal Pharoahs, those struggles that keep them enslaved, and their yearning for freedom. The discussion inevitably takes a political turn as we remember all those around the world who are still in bondage, asking ourselves what we can and should do.

In Jerusalem that Passover of 1988, I was like those Jews in the story who were passing through the Red Sea, fleeing for their very lives. All of my energy and attention were going into survival. Survival as a woman. Survival as a Jew. Deeply discouraged and demoralized, I didn't know if I'd make it to the other side.

For some converts, the conversion itself is like crossing the Red Sea. They consider the waters of the *mikveh* to be like the waters that Moses led the people through, a passage to spiritual freedom on the other side.

For me, however, the story was different. My conversion was more like the prelude to the central drama. The orthodox shul and my search for a rabbi had certainly been trying, but my vision at that time was clear. The tightest constriction, the hardest part of becoming a Jew, my real birth, was passing through my own ambivalence raised by the issues of anti-Semitism, chauvinism, and sexism. This was my Red Sea.

Memoirs of spiritual journeys often focus on the writer's relationship with God. Visions of grandeur are recounted, and moments of despair or communion with the divine described. But my spiritual journey had a different character, embedded as it was in community and greatly affected by my feelings about it. Its most difficult moments had less to do with God and more to do with the people around me.

Because of this, I didn't recognize that I was moving

through a spiritual crisis. My growing cynicism threatened to overwhelm the tender and immediate connection I felt with the divine. No longer going to services, too busy to meditate, hardly ever alone, I lost touch with the deeper realms that had nourished me before. I felt this loss, but did not give it a name.

Just as the Jews who fled through the Red Sea could not envision the other side until they reached it, I could not imagine where I was headed. All I knew was the present, with my disillusionment and my despair. And I worried for my safety: Would I be overwhelmed and drowned in the waters?

Cracks. More cracks than I describe here. The union between Michael and me could not withstand all the erosion. The life we created together was not able to bear the burden of our dissatisfaction and anger.

One more year would pass before I left the marriage. In that time we tried desperately to heal the wounds, but they were too deep. The love between us should have been enough, but it wasn't.

The reality of a failed relationship depressed me, and I struggled with a feeling of shame. What kind of person was I? I feared that something in me was defective, that I was inadequate for any relationship.

Jewish marriages are meant to last, as the religion is built around family life. But if a marriage is too difficult, and the unhappiness too great, the health of the partners takes precedence. This understanding gave me strength, and after months of struggle, I came to the decision that I would leave.

"What about the magazine?" Michael asked in one of the saddest conversations of my life. "What are your plans?"

I thought for several moments before I answered. I had never intended to do this work for long, as my creativity as a writer could not flourish in such a setting. "I'm leaving that, too," I answered. "But not immediately. I'll stay until we get someone to replace me. You can have the magazine."

Leave the marriage? Leave the magazine? A double loss. Both of us wept.

I skip here to the beginning of 1990, a new decade. By this time I had come closer to the other side of the Red Sea, although I hadn't yet reached the shore. The passage through these waters was taking much longer than I expected.

My distress about sexism in the Jewish world slowed me down. I had experienced it everywhere in the past five years, in the Jewish organizational world, at the magazine, and in the religion itself. I went over and over these instances, reliving my painful feelings, trying to understand. But my disillusionment was great, and this issue would not be easily resolved.

Six months earlier I had left Michael, moving nearby to a little house with a garden. My work at *Tikkun* was now finished, my responsibilities divided among Michael and several staff members so that I could leave in good conscience and on good terms. Saying goodbye to the marriage and the magazine had been extremely painful. Day after day I laid on my bed, weeping, so disconsolate I didn't answer the phone when it rang.

Yet after a while I began to feel the presence of great possibility. With everything cleared away, what would emerge?

I had avoided living alone in the past, but now I welcomed it, appreciating the silence. With newfound energy I appointed my home, choosing a couch and a rug that suited me, the new me, the living-alone me. I was drawn to the color red. Bold red, rich red, subtle red. And the walls a quiet white. Sensuality and warmth against a backdrop of solitude. Pictures on the walls of places I had been, paintings of women and fruit and hillsides.

Since my teens, I had been married, or on my way to being married. Now I would explore another dimension as a single woman. I had a lot of healing to do. My weariness and despair, accumulated through my life and especially through the last few years, were all too obvious to me. In my honest moments I admitted that I had come close to collapse with the breakup of my marriage, the pressures of *Tikkun,* and my internal struggle.

Creating a home was the easiest part of my new life. Should the tiles in the bathroom be white or lilac, the kitchen floor oak or Mexican pavers? The answers came quickly. But beneath the flurry of activity, a very large question loomed: Now what?

I'd take time to write, I decided. For years I had wanted this. Going through my old journals, I came across entries from the seventies, written in a younger woman's hand, that reminded me that I had the dream of a writing life even then. Now, with my children gone and enough money to remain unemployed for a while, I finally had the opportunity.

Would I become isolated at home, writing? I feared falling into lethargy or depression. But I had picked my new neighborhood carefully, making sure that I was near a busy street and that many of my neighbors worked at home during the day. If I felt disconnected, all I needed to do was walk outside my door.

After the *Tikkun* years of political wrangling and national exposure, I could not imagine losing my connection to organized Jewish life, but it seemed tenuous without the magazine. I feared I might drift away and be forgotten. I'd keep myself involved by consulting with progressive Jewish organizations and participating on several boards, I decided. This would be my way of contributing to the community.

Soon after I moved into my new house, before I'd even begun the remodeling, I decided to hold a house-warming. In Jewish homes this celebration is called a *Hanukat HaBayit*. As part of the festivities, the new home-dwellers and their friends gather around the front door to hang the mezuzah, a small ornamental case that contains a scroll inscribed with words from the Torah. After songs and blessings, everyone helps to nail the mezuzah to the gatepost of the house.

My *Hanukat HaBayit* took place on a Sunday afternoon in early autumn. Friends from *Tikkun* and the community filled my as-yet-unfurnished living room. To my delight, my mother and a few other members of my family also came. On a big table I spread out platters of hummus and babaganoush, vegetables and pita bread, olives and pickles. A large chocolate cake stood nearby, to be cut after the mezuzah was hung. We drank wine, and the atmosphere was festive.

"It's time for the mezuzah," my friend Barry called, after a while. "Everyone gather by the door, please." As the unofficial spiritual leader of the local Jewish renewal community, he had volunteered to orchestrate this part of the celebration.

We began singing a *niggun,* and the group pressed forward so that everyone could see. "Where's the mezuzah?" Barry asked. I handed him the one I had bought the summer before in Israel. Made from Jerusalem lime-stone, it was the most beautiful in the shop, and I had wrapped it carefully in my nightgown and stuck it in the middle of my suitcase for the trip back to the States. Pale pink, gracefully shaped, it was perfect for my new home.

"I want to bless you, Nan, that this home nourish you and give you pleasure, and that your days here be filled with creativity," Barry said.

"Amen!" everyone shouted.

Several other people gave me their blessings, and together we read the traditional prayers for this occasion. After a few songs, Barry took the mezuzah and positioned it at a forty-five-degree angle on the doorpost. I took the hammer, and gently knocked the top nail in a little way. Everyone applauded.

"Who wants to go next?" Barry said. "You each get a chance." A few of my closest friends drove the nail in a little deeper, so that the mezuzah was more secure.

"What about Nan's family?" someone called. "Let them have a turn."

One of my closest relatives, an older woman, was brought to the front of the crowd. Barry handed her the hammer, and she raised it way back beyond her head. In a moment of omniscience, I knew what was going to happen next. Before I could stop her, she brought the hammer down with surprising force, smashing the mezuzah to pieces.

A gasp went through the group. The unimaginable had happened, a relative of the new homeowner breaking the mezuzah. And even more shocking, a non-Jew destroying this Jewish holy object.

I staggered under the weight of the moment, stunned, then embarrassed. My friends, who wished the best for me, didn't know what to say. Seeing their discomfort, I rushed in with reassurance. "Superglue will do the trick," I told them.

We pried the jagged pieces of the mezuzah off the doorpost and carried them into the kitchen. But when I tried to piece them together, they did not fit. "Do you have another mezuzah?" somebody asked. I didn't.

The party was in danger of collapsing under too many unspoken feelings. My relative hardly seemed to understand what had happened. "I guess I did something wrong," she said. "The hammer . . . it slipped." I couldn't answer.

"Please, everybody, I'll get another mezuzah tomorrow," I said, as my friends milled around, trying to be helpful. "Don't worry, it doesn't mean anything." But the destruction of the mezuzah had unsettled us, and although we tried to get back into a celebratory spirit, we couldn't.

After everyone left, I slowly walked from room to room in this home I already loved. The sweetness of the walls, the last rays of autumn light coming through the tall windows, and the feeling of peace reassured me. The broken mezuzah would not be a bad omen, after all.

In the kitchen I turned on the overhead light and once again tried to fit together the mezuzah shards. Less distracted than before, I concentrated on one piece, then another. Finally the mezuzah began to take shape. With the help of Superglue, enough of it stuck together so that it resembled its original form, and I left it to dry overnight.

The next morning, when I picked it up, it cracked in two in my hands, but this was an improvement over the day before. Outside, on my doorpost, I gently hammered the top half of the mezuzah into place, then the bottom half, wedging the scroll into the little grove inside. For good measure I smeared superglue over the entire surface, making sure that the edges adhered to the wooden doorpost. Standing back, I looked with satisfaction at my new mezuzah. It lit up my doorway.

Later that day the man who was in charge of the remodeling job at my house stopped by. An orthodox Jew, he immediately noticed my mezuzah. "What happened here?" he asked.

"Oh, it broke," I answered, as though this were the most ordinary occurrence. "I glued it together."

"Well," he hesitated, "I'm sorry to tell you, but it's upside down."

"Oh, no!" In my determination to mount it on my doorpost, I somehow had lost track of direction. Now I noticed that the Hebrew letters were facing the wrong way.

"You should have used screws," he continued. "They're better than nails."

"You're right." My pleasure with my mezuzah was fading quickly.

"I'll take it down for you. Then you can replace it," he said.

This was too much. My fierce attachment to my mezuzah returned. "Thanks, but I'm satisfied with it the way it is."

I knew that he did not approve, but I didn't care. My broken mezuzah stayed in place, upside down, for two more years, until I found another I liked almost as much. When I pried off the original one, the paint from the doorpost came with it, the remains of the Superglue. Until then, I was reminded of that housewarming whenever I came through my front door. Against great odds, my mezuzah and I had prevailed.

The experience of the mezuzah reflected one of the themes in my life. Pushing through. Persevering. Overcoming. Certainly this had been the story of the last several years, beginning with my conversion. The mezuzah's presence on the doorpost was evidence that I was a woman who survived. Proud of this identity, I considered it to be one of my strongest qualities.

But I sensed the danger of living my life only on this level. Seeing the world through the lens of survival meant that I was driven by will and governed by pride. What would I be if other aspects of myself came to the foreground, and how would my experience change? There were lessons to be learned, and I knew they would come.

I settled into my new life alone, working on a novel and consulting with other magazines during the days, going to meetings or seeing friends and family in the evenings. Although I continued to mourn the loss of my marriage and the magazine, this period was marked by discovery. How easy to have no one to worry about but myself. How easy to eat when I wanted, go where I wished.

I reveled in this freedom, but with freedom came decisions. Looming over everything was the question of what kind of Jew I was going to be. I had made a lifetime commitment to Judaism, but I didn't know where I'd fall on the scale between religious and secular. Did I want to observe Shabbat and *kashrut*? What about services? And scariest of all, what about my heart's connection to Judaism?

Even before I separated from Michael, I had begun to question leading a traditional Jewish life. Did it really matter if Shabbat started on time, or that I observed it by *davvening*? I seemed to get as much out of going for a hike in the hills on Saturday morning.

Emotionally, I was ready to explore a less rigid Judaism. But what did this mean as a convert? If I moved too far away from a traditional Jewish practice, would I be in danger of slipping back over the ethnic divide? I didn't have Jewish blood to secure my identity, after all.

I also worried about my appearance as a Jew. Despite the mezuzah on my door, I was a convert living alone, without a Jewish family. This already made me suspect in the eyes of many traditional Jews. I imagined their voices: "No family? This is a Jew?" In the past, when the subject of divorced women converts was raised, I had overheard these women's Jewish credentials being seriously challenged. "Just watch. She converted to marry, but now that she's divorced, she'll go back to the *goyim*."

It wasn't only religious Jews who made assumptions about converts living alone. One afternoon, a year after I moved into my new home, Tara, a secular Jew, came by to see me. She had worked at the *Tikkun* office for a brief time, and she wanted a recommendation for a new job.

After we made arrangements, she hesitated at the door. "I was just wondering about you," she said. "Are you still Jewish?"

Her question took me by surprise. "Of course. Why wouldn't I be?"

"I thought, with your divorce. . . . Now that you're no longer with Michael. . . . "

She could have said more, but I didn't want to hear it. "Once a Jew, always a Jew," I laughed, although I knew my statement didn't hold for some people, including secular people like herself. "Seriously, yes, I'm Jewish. It's the center of my life."

"Good," she replied, and we parted.

The center of my life? I had said this, but was it really true? By this time my level of observance had dramatically dropped. On Shabbat I still lit candles, although this, too, would soon stop. But no sooner were they lit than I'd put them on the tiled hearth so they'd be safe, and run out the door to a film or to dinner in a restaurant with a friend. And by the time Saturday arrived, I didn't think much about Shabbat, as I had errands to do, or the latest museum exhibition, or a sale at a favorite clothing store.

Shabbat was not the only Jewish observance that was slipping away. *Kashrut* also had less meaning, as I questioned its importance.

One weekday evening, in an upscale restaurant with my mother, I glanced over the menu. "I'll have the roast beef," I said.

"Roast beef? You?" She looked at me with great disbelief, then a smile broke over her face. "That makes me happy. Now you're getting back to being yourself."

I wanted that roast beef more than anything; I could already taste its salty juices, feel its chewy texture in my mouth. And I wanted to give her something, too. Despite the tension that existed between us because of my conversion, I wished to be closer to her. Now that I was less careful about what I ate, now that I didn't ask about every ingredient when I went to restaurants, I could do this for her. But roast beef? This was my first nonkosher meat in years.

"I'm every bit as Jewish," I said, drawing the line.

"I see," she nodded, her eyes gleaming. "But it sounds like you're getting tired of it."

"No, it's not that at all," I replied. "There are many ways to be Jewish. I just don't want to be so observant anymore." I knew she would not grasp what I said, but in that moment I didn't need her to reflect my understanding. It was enough that something between us softened, and when she slipped her arm through mine as we went out of the restaurant, I felt great tenderness.

It didn't take long for the whole family to hear about our dinner. "Grandma told me you had roast beef," my daughter laughed.

"Did she tell you that I'm just as Jewish?" I answered.

"Not really."

"Well, I am." I didn't bother to explain to my daughter the fine points of my Jewish observance. Over the last several years she had openheartedly accepted me as a Jew, but she wasn't interested in the details.

"At least it will make family dinners easier if you aren't kosher," she said.

"We'll see," I answered. I imagined my mother plying me with ham or bacon. When I refused, which I would because I had decided I wouldn't eat pork, we'd enter the same difficult territory. Only she'd have the added ammunition of reminding me that I had ordered roast beef in her presence and enjoyed every bite.

I was making a new life, becoming more secular, heading down an unconventional path. Converts typically have great enthusiasm for Judaism, more than most other Jews. Religious Jews are suspicious of this, and secular Jews consider it stupidity or naiveté. Still, an enthusiastic convert is easier for Jews to understand than a convert who develops a critical attitude.

The biblical character Ruth embodies the ideal vision of the convert in traditional Judaism. "Your people are my people," she said to her Jewish mother-in-law Naomi, as they journeyed together to the land of Canaan. Dutiful and devoted to the Jewish people, the convert Ruth did everything right. She was as good as good could be, the best yet, and in the end the lineage of King David sprang from her.

I wanted to be good: this had been the role I had adopted during my lifetime. My high school graduation picture shows a young woman, calm and composed, no trouble to anyone, a churchgoing person, hair carefully curled, lipstick and smile in place, eyes guarded. Being good was my first impulse, the safest way I knew, my hedge against harm.

Yet now the expectation of goodness as a convert felt confining, and I strained against it. I didn't want to be better than other Jews, the perfect Ruth. My Jewish friends had the freedom to doubt and complain, rebel and reject. If chunks of the religion were unacceptable to them, they cut them out. Why shouldn't that be my right? I was as Jewish as they were, so I should be able to deviate from the traditional path without guilt or censure.

The center was holding. I had been right when I told Tara that Judaism was the center of my life. Only the form was changing, as I was drawn more and more in a secular direction.

Secular Judaism. During my orthodox years, I had heard many nasty comments about secular Jews. Betrayers of the tradition and abandoners of the people, it was said. Their attachment to Judaism existed only through lox and bagels. And their way of life inevitably led to intermarriage, investigation of other religions, and eventual rejection of Jewish identity.

But I never believed this. In my experience I had known too many committed secular Jews who organized their lives around Jewish values, even though they weren't religious. When we started *Tikkun,* many of these people contacted us. Therapists, activists, healers of all kinds, artists and creators, thinkers and doers, people who wanted to change the world. In the opinion of traditional Jews these people were hardly Jewish, as they did not observe the religion or involve themselves in the religious community, but I knew their commitment to politics came from their Jewish heritage.

Secular Judaism was a familiar, comfortable world for me. When I lived in the Midwest in my twenties with my Protestant husband and children, my two closest women friends were secular Jews, red-diaper babies. We often drank coffee around the kitchen table while our children played in the backyard. The setting was conventional, but the conversation was not. We critically analyzed American culture and politics, and talked with sorrow about the oppression in the world. None of us "believed in God," as we put it, and we were all committed to political action to "change the system."

The sixties were brewing in our quiet Midwest city. My friends and I organized anti-HUAC meetings and went to demonstrations protesting the Vietnam War. Late at night, after our children fell asleep, we'd sit around on big pillows, playing the guitar and singing folk songs with our husbands. My friends would tell stories about their Jewish immigrant parents and grandparents, and how they fought for justice all their lives. I felt envious of this heritage, and considered it higher, purer than my own.

After my Jewish friends and I had known each other a few years, we became an extended family, with our children and spouses. In the self-conscious way of the sixties, we carefully defined our extended-family life: separate homes for each family, frequent communal meals, shared child care.

Holidays were special times. The most satisfying holiday of all was Passover. It not only had good food, it had political meaning. For the seder we used a radical nonreligious order of service, a *hagaddah* we found in *Ramparts* magazine. New to this holiday, I quickly learned "*Dayenu*," a boisterous Hebrew Passover song, and sang it with my extended family as though it had been mine for a lifetime.

My friends were secular in a way that was a teaching to me. They embraced their heritage wholeheartedly, proud to be Jews. They did not feel a contradiction between their Jewish identity and their secular commitment to fight for justice. Quite the opposite, their activism sprang from their heritage.

When I met my friends' relatives, I found they shared these same values. One wintry weekend I traveled to Washington, D.C., to march in the Jeanette Rankin Brigade against the Vietnam War. Barbara, a member of my extended family, came with me, and her mother, an outspoken veteran of many battles, met us there. In this woman's mind she had no choice as a secular Jew but to protest an unjust war, so she had risen at dawn and taken the bus from New York, silver flask of Cherry-Heering stashed in her purse as protection against the cold.

I felt at home with these people. Having grown up in a family that was apolitical, I learned from my extended family how to live a life committed to social justice. The Christianity I knew in the fifties had not given me this. As I became more comfortable as an activist, I felt more alive. Rather than being a spectator, I was now connected to all humanity, contributing to its betterment.

Religious Jews would consider the people in my extended family less than Jewish, but I saw them as deeply rooted in the tradition. True, I was a Christian, looking in. But my secular friends' passion and their perseverance seemed, and still seems, as Jewish to me as the religious devotion of orthodox men who attend the morning minyan.

* * *

When I lived alone in my new house after the breakup of my marriage to Michael, most of my friends were secular Jews. I was a curiosity among them.

"Why did you convert, anyway?" Sandy asked one night when a few of us had gathered. "Judaism is such a patriarchal religion."

Explaining that I had been drawn spiritually to the religion, I could see by her expression she didn't understand. "As a feminist . . ." she began. "How could you?"

"It's a problem," I replied.

Marcia, another friend, broke into the conversation. "Nan's a special case. She's the only person I know who converted because of Jewish culture. Forget religion, she's an ethnic convert."

"Right!" I answered, glad to get off the hook of explaining a paradox that still mystified me, even though Marcia's assessment was only part of the story. "My first deep connection with Judaism came through my secular Jewish extended family. I learned a lot from them," I told Sandy.

"See, she's ethnic," Marcia laughed.

Sandy still seemed perplexed, but for now, she shook her head and looked at Marcia and me lovingly. "Okay, if you say so."

My friends liked to speculate about why I converted, but they seemed to accept me as a secular Jew. Thus I was not prepared for what happened later when seven of us went away on a weekend retreat. Late one night we were sprawled on couches, relaxed from the wine we'd been drinking, watching the light from the fire dance over the walls of our rented beach cottage.

"A lot of us here are Jewish," one of the women said.

"I just realized it." We all laughed, as though she had made a joke.

Laura, one of the Jews, began to count: "One, two, three, four," she pointed at those born Jewish.

I waited patiently to see if I would be included. I wasn't. "What about me?" I asked.

My four Jewish-born friends considered the question. "Well, maybe there's four-and-a-half Jews here," one of them finally said, and they laughed loudly. I laughed too, but I was stung by their response.

The next day I questioned them. They hardly remembered the incident, although for me it had colored the whole evening. Seeing that I was still upset, they did their best to reassure me.

"You're one of us," Laura said. "Of course you're Jewish."

"Of course," I replied. I wanted to believe she meant it, but I was left hanging on the giddy edge of paranoia. Did the wine make her and the others more truthful the night before, or was she now saying what she really thought?

This incident made me realize the strangeness of my position as a secular Jew. I couldn't blame my friends for being confused. When we discussed the issues of patriarchy and sexism in Judaism, I was as angry as they. "I can't stand to go to services anymore," I said. "The language bothers me too much, with all the male references."

I was an anomaly, a woman who chooses Judaism and rejects large parts of it. Yet within the tradition, there is room for people like me. Jews are not required to believe in God and go to services. The core of being a Jew is commitment to the Jewish people, an ethnic identification. I certainly had that.

Besides, converts are full-fledged Jews, whether we

are religious or not. As long as our conversions were done according to Jewish law, we remain Jews until we die. If we were to convert to another religion or disavow our affiliation, we wouldn't be considered Jewish by the community. But no formal court exists to expel converts, or reject us from the faith.

Although my behavior confounded others, I knew it to be part of an important process. In 1991 an idea started to crystalize in my mind: I had become like a fallow field. This seventh year after I began the formal process of conversion, I was taking time off from Judaism to become rejuvenated. I was giving myself a sabbatical.

The Torah commands Jews to let the land rest every seventh year, just as God rested after six days of creation. The earth accumulates dredge and silt, and underneath its unkept surface, insects burrow and minerals collect, allowing it to grow fertile for the years ahead.

Nothing appears to be happening when a field is fallow, but this period is part of the creative process. I've had the experience of not even thinking about a writing project before I begin, busying myself by reading the newspaper or going for a walk. But once I'm involved in the project, I understand how crucial the fallow state has been.

For a field to be fallow, it must be returned to the elements. Thus, I abandoned my attempt to control my spiritual journey. Trusting that something would grow from the soil of my soul, I let go of trying to settle my relationship to Judaism and the Jewish people.

The choice of a biblical image to describe a retreat from the religion was ironic, I realized. The split between my attachment to Judaism and my detachment was only too evident. But the image gave me comfort. Fields do not stay fallow for long.

When I am angry, my heart is closed. This state of being separates me from spiritual experience, and cuts me off from the mystery of the divine.

In my fallow-field years, from 1990 to 1993, I did not fully grasp the connection between emotion and spirituality. But I felt the presence of great anger about sexism, and knew it was keeping me from spiritual growth.

My negativity toward Judaism seemed to be the most obvious expression of this anger. Pronounced and sharp, it sprang up whenever I thought about male God language, or the proliferation of male images in the liturgy, or the historical exclusion of women from the texts. In my introspective moments I realized that my anger was not just about the patriarchal aspects of Judaism. The larger anger had to do with my feelings about men, and most specifically about my father.

When my father died unexpectedly in 1990, I grieved. The tension between us had never been resolved, and I was left to sort through it alone. I felt a great deal of rage at him for the way he had alienated himself from our family and for the way he lived his last years. Some of this feeling was displaced onto Judaism. It was much easier to rail about orthodox inequality or sexist language in the liturgy than to descend to the layers of pain that existed in my relationship with him.

My attachment to my father was strong. Throughout my adult life I sought out charismatic men like him, repeating the pattern of our relationship. No wonder, then, that I had chosen Judaism, a religion that is patriarchal in its core. The strong presence of men reassured me. Here I could experience once again the familiar combination of great possibility and great disappointment. My personal issues with my father and other men could be played out on the larger screen of spiritual struggle.

I needed to attend to my feelings of anger and pain, experiencing their force so that I could let them go. Until I did this, I would stay in a spiritually contracted state.

In my fallow-field period, I began to focus on these feelings, writing in my journal, taking long walks alone, and talking with a few close friends. This helped. But the deepest healing seemed to come from being with women. The feminine, the mother, finally moved into the center of my consciousness.

I had not planned for this to happen. I only knew I wanted to be with women in a more open way. Cautiously at first, then enthusiastically, I sought them out, making new friends, joining a women's group that meets to this day, involving myself in women's organizations and political activities.

Women became the foreground in my emotional world, men the background. When I arrived at a benefit for a Jewish theater group during this period, I scanned the room, deciding who I wanted to meet. I chose only women, although in the past I would have gravitated toward men, soliciting their attention.

In conversations, at parties, at meetings with women, my talents seemed to be appreciated, my words understood. Here I could speak about my frustrations as a woman, and heads would nod in agreement. My experience certainly was not unique.

In my women's group, my sense of self expanded. Not only was I seen as a nurturing person, but I was respected for the way my mind worked and the integrity of my opinions. This affirmation strengthened me, so that I became even more sure of myself.

I do not intend to idealize the women's community. Women struggle with competition and envy as much as men. But within this community I found the support I needed to heal the anger within.

Some of my anger in the past had come from a feeling of powerlessness in the face of men's determination. Now I discovered I needed to look more carefully at myself. Since I seldom associated with men during this period, I could not blame them anymore for every unhappiness I suffered. I had to acknowledge my part of the responsibility.

Over time I began to view men and the Jewish patriarchy with measured compassion. I still saw the damage that had been done to the souls of women, but I no longer felt interested in retribution. Men were wounded, as was I, and hampered by the constraints of their roles. Something needed to be done for all of us to be freed from this prison.

I cannot write about my experience in the women's community without including my relationship with Susan. In many ways this relationship embodied the healing I received. During that period of working through my feelings about men, Susan and I met. We were drawn to each other, and after a while we became lovers.

When I converted to Judaism, I knew that I would be a Jew until I died. But I was not sure of my future sexual identity when I became involved with Susan. The relationship was more an expression of my desire to be close to her than a statement of sexual identity. As a result, I did not feel that I was declaring myself in the way some women do when they have struggled with this issue for a lifetime, knowing that a lesbian identity is the fullest description of their being.

My family's attitude helped to make my passage into this relationship with Susan easier. They accepted it with equanimity. Since other members of the family were gay, it caused far less distress than my becoming Jewish. Besides, we had all been through a painful time with my conversion, and nobody seemed to want to cause further strain.

Susan's Anglo-Saxon heritage reassured my family. With her fair hair, rounded features, and blue eyes, she could have been a relative. Her presence in my life was a return to familiar ground for my family, as well as for me.

Living in an open-minded community also made this transition smoother. Although a great deal of prejudice exists against gays and lesbians in the Jewish world, the progressive left flank embraces gay rights. In my work with these progressive organizations, I spoke comfortably about my connection to Susan. People asked about her as they would about a husband or a child, acknowledging her importance in my life.

One night Rabbi Zalman was slated to appear at the local Hillel center with Rabbi Shlomo Carlebach, the beloved musician and teacher. They were to have a public dialogue about their experience as spiritual leaders over the last four decades, and I invited Susan to come.

The meeting hall was filled with these men's admirers and students, and the air crackled with excitement. When Zalman came through the door, everyone cheered.

"Greetings, all of you," he said, taking the microphone. "I'm so glad to be here. We'll wait a few minutes to begin, until Shlomo comes." The crowd laughed, knowing that Rabbi Shlomo always arrived hours late.

People surrounded Zalman, and in his usual way, he warmly embraced them. I stayed at a distance. There would be plenty of time later to introduce Susan to him.

After a while Zalman waved at me. "Nan, hello!" he shouted. "Come over here!"

Susan and I pushed our way through the crowd to where he stood. "*Mazel tov*! I hear good things about the two of you," he said, smiling into our eyes.

He wanted to give us a blessing. Taking our hands in his big hands, closing his eyes, rocking back and forth, he said, "I bless you, Nan and Susan, that you find what you are looking for in this relationship. That you learn what you need to learn. . . . " On he went, but I could not hear him above the noise. Overcome by his kindness, my eyes filled with tears.

"Thanks, Zalman," I whispered, when he finished.

With this kind of support, it was easy to be with Susan in the Jewish community. But Zalman was an exceptional rabbi. Word reached me later that the rabbi from the East Coast who had performed my orthodox conversion on my wedding day was horrified by the course my life had taken.

"I never should have converted her," he told someone. "It was a very big mistake." He went on to say that he wished he could annul the conversion.

This information saddened me. Despite the pain of the orthodox conversion, I appreciated the effort of this rabbi. He had gone out of his way for me, and I was sorry to disappoint him.

But his reaction did not surprise me. Homosexuality is condemned in orthodox Judaism, and interfaith relationships are not acceptable. I had more than enough marks against me to be considered a complete failure as a convert.

Although I understood the orthodox rabbi's position, it also made me angry. "I'm still the same person," I imagined saying. "I was good enough for you when I was a Jewish wife, but now you reject me? This is not right." I presented my case, listing all my work in Jewish organizations, telling him how much I cared about the Jewish people, how committed I was. In my imagination the rabbi listened for a moment, then turned slightly away.

Spiritual paths often take unpredictable turns. The relationship with Susan gave me a setting to more fully experience myself as a Jew. After six years of struggling for acceptance in the Jewish community, and after being married to a man who was far more knowledgeable than I about Judaism, I liked being the one in our relationship with the Jewish credentials.

Susan and I often discussed Judaism and spirituality. Even though we both came from Christian families, our experiences were very different. She had been exposed to it at a much earlier age. As a teenager she had lived with a secular Jewish family that became her legal guardians after her father died. This family was critical of religion but taught her a love of Jewish culture and introduced her to *Yiddishkeit*. In subsequent years she considered conversion, but decided against it because of her discomfort with institutionalized religious structures. Now she was a Buddhist.

In this interfaith relationship I realized even more the importance of my conversion to Judaism. I was a Jew, and she was not. This difference between us stood out as we negotiated our way through issues that interfaith couples typically face. What about Christmas? As a Jew, I didn't want anything to do with it because of its historical connection to Christianity, but Susan saw it as a pagan holiday and loved celebrating it, remembering times of warmth from her childhood. Although we tried to accommodate both our feelings, neither of us was entirely satisfied.

My life as an orthodox Jew was hard to explain to Susan, because it was so far from her own experience. But we often talked about our culturally similar childhoods. For the last six years I had concentrated on my Jewish self, and now I was ready to further integrate the Christian cultural side. Susan helped me with this. Through her I became reacquainted with the disavowed past, accepting it as part of my experience. I could not have done this if I hadn't already established myself as a Jew. And it would have been impossible if I didn't have faith in my own spiritual path.

The relationship with Susan provided something even more precious, the space to sort out my feelings about being Jewish. I'd often sit in the big white chair in my living room late at night, considering my experience. After all the words about Judaism in the past, after all the talk about the Jewish community at *Tikkun*, the silence soothed me.

Left alone with Judaism, I could acknowledge what was deepest in my heart. In the quiet of the night, I let the feelings come. Love. Disappointment. Appreciation. Despair. Only I could own them all, and only I could find reconciliation.

And then the yearning began. Enough healing had taken place for me to feel it. One Friday evening I was on my way out the door to a birthday party, and I passed by the Shabbat candlesticks. To my surprise, I experienced an overwhelming feeling of yearning, flooding through my body, leaving me limp. Only with great effort did I pull myself away.

Another Saturday I drove by the little orthodox shul while services were going on. No one was outside, so I parked in front. Through my open window I strained to hear the singing. When the melodious *"Adon Olam"* began, I sang it softly, then louder, weeping, my heart filled with longing. How could I be separated from this beauty? I sat there until the first congregants spilled out the door, and then I drove away, my heart racing.

This yearning, so palpable, rose in me from time to time. It washed over my being, leaving me breathless, teary. I felt a deep sadness. But I also felt its sweetness. Just beyond desire was the sweetness of possibility.

And so I waited, still the fallow field, experiencing this emotion, even treasuring it. I knew that it was a sign that the field was readying itself to bring forth life once again.

I was not a stranger to spiritual yearning. Twenty years before, it had first appeared. I was living in the Midwest at the time, busy with my psychotherapy practice, raising my children, studying at the university.

An atheist, I had no interest in the spiritual dimension of life. But in the hundred-mile commute to the university, my only time alone, I began to experience this same feeling of yearning. Like now, it came as an intense wave of longing. Sometimes I had to pull my car to the side of the freeway until I recovered.

This feeling frightened me. I did not know that it was the prelude to what would be one of the strongest spiritual experiences of my life. Instead, I worried that I was falling apart, and I sought an explanation in psychology.

Still the yearning continued. Even when I was with others, it hovered in the background. I began to sense that it was existential in nature, profound rather than pathological. It pointed the way somewhere, but I did not know where.

One day in 1979, while working in my psychotherapy office with a woman client, I had an experience that astonished me. My client was talking about a problem at her school for retarded students, a usual topic for her. Suddenly I became aware of an incredible force existing in that room, a love greater than human love. So powerful was it that even the light in the room changed, becoming clear and white. My client did not seem to notice, but I felt a radiance within me and around me I had not known before.

The intensity of this experience was soon over, but it lingered for hours. What had happened? Later I recognized that the experience had been spiritual, but that day in my office I felt confused. Wasn't I a secular person, an atheist? I had not asked for this.

As the months went by, this experience happened again in my work, at home, when I was alone or with others. I did not dare say anything about it, because those close to me would not have understood.

Still, I came to welcome these experiences. Being bathed in divine love was a lot better than the pain of yearning, which had mysteriously receded. The question remained, however. Was this God? It certainly was different from the father-in-the-sky God of my childhood, but it had the unmistakable feel of holiness. I didn't know what to call it, but I remembered those times long ago when I went to the creek, and found there the feeling of union with all of life.

"Perhaps spirituality is valid," I heard myself saying at a meeting of psychotherapists in the early eighties. We were "grouping," as it was called, talking about our lives, and I ventured this idea.

"Maybe," somebody answered, and that was the extent of interest in a possibility that seemed so revolutionary to me.

More and more, I experienced this spiritual dimension as real and accessible. But I began to feel lonely. I wanted to share it with others. I thought of Grandma Alice and how she found a community of like-minded people in her church. My experience didn't seem Christian, however. And I had no interest in returning to the church.

In my mind only one possibility existed: Judaism. How I came to this conclusion, I do not know. I don't remember a definitive moment, an "Aha!" experience. I simply slid into the recognition that this was the place for me. I had been circling the Jewish community for years, loving it, appreciating its values, connecting on the secular level, creating an extended family with secular Jews, but now, with this spiritual awakening, I was ready to become a Jew myself.

It would take a few more years for me to move to California and begin the formal process of converting. Although I continued to feel lonely, I was comforted by the presence of this divine love. It was not constant; sometimes it went away for weeks, even months, but it always returned.

When I finally arrived at the orthodox shul in California, I thought I had reached the end of the journey that began with yearning. Joining in the prayers and the singing, I no longer felt alone. Even though I didn't know Hebrew, I could sink into the familiar state of love in the presence of others who were experiencing a similar consciousness. Together we were connecting to the holiness beyond ourselves.

In the months that followed, my Hebrew improved and I became familiar with the prayers. The amount of learning was immense. A great body of Jewish liturgy exists, and each prayer is shaded with layers of meanings. Religious Jews pray three times a day, each service with its own prayers. And the customs around prayer—when to stand, when to sit, when to bow, when to sing, when to pray aloud, when to be silent—these take years of learning.

Visitors to more traditional Jewish religious services are often astounded by all the words. Pages and pages of them, spoken or sung rapid-fire, seemingly without thought. How can anyone's mind keep up? It can't, and that's the point. The liturgy potentially acts as a vehicle to transport the congregants to a closeness with the divine. It is a form of meditation that fills the consciousness so that external thoughts are driven out. There's no time to think, although of course the mind wanders in the midst of liturgy, just as it does with any form of meditation.

In those early days at the orthodox shul, I intuitively understood this. The orthodox setting gave me what I needed spiritually. But as I became disillusioned with orthodoxy and grew to reject the male language of the liturgy, the connection could not sustain me. I'd found my way to the right religion, but it would take a while longer to settle into a place that was right for me.

Now, in this seventh year after my conversion, I was back in a state of yearning. As had happened before, the feeling came upon me at unexpected times. I didn't fear I was losing my mind, as I had in the Midwest, but it disturbed me.

This yearning was the prelude to my next spiritual step as a Jew. On the intuitive level I knew this. When I remembered where it had led me twenty years ago, to that startling first experience with the divine in my psychotherapy office, I felt reassured.

But I still had questions. Perhaps my yearning really came from a deeper dissatisfaction with Judaism than I had acknowledged. If this were so, what would I do? I had gone as far as I could within Judaism. I had studied the religion and followed all the observances, and I'd been to more services than most Jews. Where else within the religion could I find meaning?

I had reached a painful point in my spiritual journey. My longing increased, but I had no hope that I would find what I needed in Judaism.

One evening when I was home alone, I pulled my Jewish Bible from the shelf and put it on the table with the Shabbat candlesticks. I looked at these objects for several minutes, then I began to touch them, stroking them with my fingertips, trying to break down the distance in the way a lover becomes close through lovemaking.

But it did not work. Instead, I felt disinterest and put the objects away. What was to become of me? I no longer had the inspiration to reconnect. I thought of my many Jewish friends who had found a spiritual home in Buddhism. When they spoke of the wisdom they received, I envied their satisfaction. But I wasn't drawn to Buddhism. I had made enough changes for one lifetime, and if Judaism didn't satisfy me spiritually, then I would have to accept its limitations.

In this state of resignation, I continued to lead my life. Still a Jew, always a Jew, even if I had given up hope of spiritual fulfillment. I planned to remain faithful to my identity, even though I felt great sadness.

But I did not stay this way for long.

The shift began one day in 1993 when I received a request from Miriam, a friend whose husband Irving was critically ill. Miriam had been an activist within the Jewish political establishment for years. She and her family were secular Jews, but with Irving dying, she wondered what to do about the memorial service.

Her first thought was for somebody to lead the *kaddish,* the traditional Hebrew prayer of mourners. Nobody in the family knew how to do it, and my name had been suggested. Miriam thought it was a good idea.

Although I hardly knew Irving, Miriam had been a great support during the *Tikkun* days. She used to keep track of me, calling and giving advice. "You're making a big mistake," she'd begin. Or, "Keep up the fight." Her timing was impeccable; I'd hear from her when I most needed an infusion of this warrior's energy.

Now she needed me. Although I was unsure of my Hebrew, I agreed to help her. I could do the *kaddish,* at least.

On the day of the memorial service, about eighty people gathered in Miriam's spacious home, high on a hill in San Francisco. When I arrived, the guests were talking in subdued tones and eating from the platters of food laid out on the long dining room table. I had with me a copy of an atheist's translation into English of the *kaddish,* as well as the traditional prayer in Hebrew. I planned to say them both.

As I came through the door, Miriam's adult daughter announced, "The rabbi's here." Everyone turned to look.

"I'm not a rabbi," I whispered.

"Yes, you are. You're our rabbi," she replied in all seriousness.

I didn't want to argue. If they needed me as their rabbi, so it would be. Later I learned that the tradition sanctions this response. If somebody calls you rabbi, you are supposed to accept that designation, because it comes straight from the heart.

With the title of rabbi, however, came responsibility. It didn't take me long to discover what it was. "Who's doing the memorial service?" I asked the oldest son.

"Aren't you?" he answered. "You're the rabbi."

"I thought I was just doing the *kaddish*," I replied, although I could see by his expression that this was about to change.

In a hurry I put together a memorial service, asking family members and friends to speak about Irving. The rest I could handle myself. Thankfully I knew more about Judaism and the Jewish tradition than those in that room.

The service flowed beautifully, with singing and readings, and prayers and memories of Irving. After the last song was over, people came up to me. "It was just perfect, rabbi. Thank you so much." A feeling of unreality hit me then, and I could just smile.

Two years later, when Miriam died, this scenario was repeated, only the crowd was several times larger and the memorial service had to be held at the Reform Temple because of space. "You're our rabbi," the family said, insisting I do the service. "We won't have it any other way."

I had been claimed by this family as their Jewish spiritual guide at a time when my connection to Judaism seemed to be dissolving. The gesture moved me deeply. But what did it mean? It was a sign, I decided. I was being pulled back in, despite my despair.

Another incident made me think about signs. For a few years I had stayed away from the Jewish bookstore, having lost my interest in studying about Judaism. But one foggy evening, I had the impulse to drop by.

"Hey, welcome back," David, the owner, called. "I've missed you."

"Thanks," I answered, pleased to be recognized.

I wandered through the aisles, reaching the section on conversion. The books were the same as I remembered, few in number. But I was reminded of the past, of the struggle to become Jewish and how much it meant to me, and my eyes filled with tears. I felt once again the stirrings of a possible return.

Just as I was ready to leave, I noticed a new book on the checkout stand, *Words on Fire: One Woman's Journey into the Sacred,* by Vanessa Ochs. Thumbing through it, I saw that this woman had not abandoned her search to find meaning within Judaism, even though she seemed as disillusioned and questioning as I was.

I would find courage here, I decided. Without even noticing, I was gathering strength for the spiritual unfolding that was soon to come.

"Don't stay away so long," David said, as I bought the book.

"I won't," I answered.

The purchase of the book was an indication of my heart opening once again to Judaism. Another took place a few months later.

In the fall of 1993 I accompanied a friend to New York on her book tour, and we stayed at a midtown hotel. This hotel had an ominous feeling, with shadowy postmodernist furnishings and dark lighting. In the lobby several muscular men, the security guards, stood with arms crossed, tattoos displayed.

"They scare me," I said to my friend. She laughed, not understanding that I was serious.

What was I doing at this hotel? This was not my New

York. "I'm going uptown," I told her, frantic to reconnect with the part of the city where I felt at home.

By this time Michael had moved the *Tikkun* office to New York from California, a move that boded well for the visibility of the magazine. We had not seen each other for a few years, not since he left California, but I headed straight for the Upper West Side, where the new office was located. Passing by the little shops, I remembered all the visits there during the *Tikkun* days, the trips to different shuls, the weekends at friends' apartments, the lectures and conferences.

When I walked through the door of the *Tikkun* office, my emotions were running high. "I can't believe it!" Michael said. "You're really here?" We self-consciously embraced, then went into his inner office, sitting together on the couch. For a while we exchanged news about children and work.

"So how are you, really?" he asked.

"Good," I answered bravely. "My life is going well, but . . . I miss all this." Tears filled my eyes, and I was so choked up I could not speak. Perhaps he thought I meant only the magazine, but I knew it was everything—the Jewish life, the Jewish atmosphere, the sense of purpose that drew us together.

"We're having a big *Tikkun* conference here in New York soon," he said. "Do you want to speak at it?"

"Yes," I answered, gratefully. Immediately we began to make plans, a safe ground.

As I left the office, I was in a daze. I hadn't expected the visit at *Tikkun* to end up with my becoming involved, but it seemed appropriate. I had missed the magazine terribly, more than I had acknowledged, and appearing at this next conference was a good way to reconnect.

A few months later, on a freezing winter day, I stood in front of the audience of 1,000 at Columbia University: "I am Nan Fink," I said. "In 1985, I founded *Tikkun*, along with Michael. These days I am not much involved in the magazine, but my heart is with it. I am the parent who watches from a distance as my child makes its way in the world. I am so pleased to be back." With these words, I began the opening address.

In traditional Judaism women have fewer religious obligations than men. The reasoning is that they must be available to care for the family. Feeding hungry children or diapering a baby takes precedence over saying prayers.

But when it comes to Shabbat, traditional women are given a very important obligation, lighting the Shabbat candles. Through this act they bring the light of Shabbat into the household, separating the holy day from the week.

Men sometimes light Shabbat candles in nontraditional homes, but I've always thought of this ritual as belonging to women. Women embody spirit in a deep way, and through the centuries, around the world, they have made the connection between the daily acts of caretaking and the sacred.

When I began to move spiritually toward Judaism again, my first act was to light the candles. Even though this was an obvious choice, it was not planned. As so often happens when a person is ready, it came about in a simple way.

One Friday evening in 1993 I was waiting for a houseguest to get ready to go out to dinner. The light of sunset filled my living room, and I watched as it softened into darkness. The familiar yearning began. It had been two years since I last lit the Shabbat candles. Suddenly the realization came to me that it was time to do it again.

I could have asked my Gentile friend to join me in this ritual, but this was my tradition, not hers, and I wanted to do it alone. Propping two short white candles into the bronze candlesticks, I struck a match. As the light from the candles took hold, I drew it toward me, feeling my body let go as it washed over me, and then I covered my eyes and said the blessing in the Hebrew feminine: *"Aht bruchah Shekhinah, Elateinu chai ha-olamim, asher kidshahtnu b'mitzvotayha, v'tzivahtnu l'hadlik ner shel Shabbat."*

Once again I was connecting to the wellspring of Jewish spirituality. I sighed deeply, letting out the tension of my ambivalence. The power of the experience cannot be expressed. Even though it lasted only a few minutes, it could have been hours.

I knew that I would light the candles every Friday evening from then on. This was not a decision that came from will, but an acknowledgment of what I needed to do. If I left future candle-lighting to chance, if I didn't make it an ongoing spiritual practice, I would not have the feeling of connection I desired. It was as clear as that.

That night, waiting for my houseguest to finish dressing, I decided that I would open myself up once again to Judaism. Despite the difficulties I had experienced, I wouldn't let it go. It was too precious. With the lighting of those candles, I settled myself back into Judaism in a new way. I had converted seven years ago, but now I was recommitting myself.

Afterward, I didn't forget. Nothing much changed at first, but each Friday I found a way to make the shift from the week into Shabbat. The difference wasn't noticeable; I still went out with friends on Friday evenings. But marking the Shabbat in this most elemental way gave me a feeling of authenticity. I was practicing what I claimed to be.

* * *

In the summer of 1993 I traveled to the south of France with another friend. We stayed in a small village along the Mediterranean coast, the most idyllic of settings. One Saturday morning, on Shabbat, I felt restless and went for a walk. The path by the pounding sea was bordered by huge boulders, and I inched my way along, the water spraying over me, the wind almost knocking me down. In a crevice among the boulders, I slipped into a private sheltered spot. There I felt the greatest desire to pray the Shabbat morning service, *Shacharit*.

I had not brought a prayer book along with me on this trip; it remained in my drawer at home, where it had been unopened for years. But I remembered the outline of the service enough so that I began it with confidence. Although I couldn't say all the words, I knew the intention of each section of the service. I could paraphrase the prayers in English, and intersperse them with the Hebrew words and melodies I remembered.

Singing in full voice, I began. "*Modah ani l'fanecha.* Thank you, God, for returning my soul to my body." On I went through the prayers, feeling the wonder of it, held by the boulders, accompanied by the sound of the ocean.

I didn't want to stop. But the service, like all Jewish services, has its own rhythm, and when it's over, it's over. "*Aleinu l'shabeach la'adon hakol.* Please, God, help us heal this world, so that everyone can live to their fullest. Amen," I sang. And then I stayed among the boulders, surrounded by their warmth, cradled by a sweet peace.

I had never before taken the service and made it so fully my own. In the past I had read and sung the words, moving into a state of meditation, but that Shabbat in France I understood something I hadn't known before: I could breathe my soul into that service, so that I was con-

226 STRANGER IN THE MIDST

nected to the tradition and present in the here and now, uniquely myself. And I could do it alone.

I had begun to discover another possibility of Jewish practice, praying by myself. But as always, in the midst of creative exploration, I didn't bother to analyze it. I felt only the rush of excitement and satisfaction that I had come anew to this service.

When I returned to the hotel room, my friend was still lounging in bed. "How was your walk?" she asked.

"Beautiful," I answered. "More beautiful than I can say."

On that trip to France, I had brought along several books about Jewish mysticism. When I travel, I like to read slowly. Away from the rush of daily life, I have the time to absorb the deeper meanings. These books on Jewish mysticism had sat for a long time on my shelf in California and now I opened them. Here was a world waiting to be explored. I was intrigued.

The Kabbalah. A hidden mystical tradition, centuries old. Part of Judaism, yet stubbornly and insistently obscure. On the highest of levels, where all mystic traditions converge, the Kabbalah exists.

Most Jews know nothing about Jewish mysticism. Through the centuries the Kabbalah was passed from chosen male to chosen male. You had to be forty and married to study it, it was said. The ideas and meditations were considered to be so powerful that a person could be destroyed by them. Even today, the Kabbalah carries the aura of danger.

Starting with the Enlightenment in the middle of the eighteenth century, the mystical tradition fell into disrepute. As Jews joined the mainstream culture, they rejected it as irrational and old-fashioned. Only the orthodox Jews in eastern Europe, and the Sephardi and Oriental Jews in northern Africa and the Middle East continued to study it. During the Holocaust much of this tradition was lost, as a high percentage of these teachers were killed.

In the last few decades, an interest in Jewish mysticism has returned. Gershom Sholem's academic work on the subject led the way, followed by other writings. Jews increasingly look to mysticism for deeper meaning. Discouraged by the spiritual emptiness they experience in their temples, synagogues, and shuls, many hunger for a way to reconnect to their heritage. If it is anywhere, they sense, it's in these teachings.

As I began to read in depth about Jewish mysticism, I hoped that I would find something in it for myself. From my studies at the yeshivah in Jerusalem before my conversion, I knew that gender in the Kabbalah is conceptualized in a surprisingly fluid way. Male and female are understood to exist in all of us. God, too, is both male and female. One of the treasured names for the divine is Shechinah, the feminine in-dwelling presence of God on earth, the holy spirit.

After my frustration with patriarchal Judaism, these ideas excited me. I knew they weren't free of sexism, as they had developed during historically patriarchal times. The masculine still was considered to be higher than the feminine, or so it seemed on first reading, but the framework was much more in line with my own thinking than the more rigid traditional Judaism. And the poetry: Soul. Spirit. Compassionate love. Reincarnation. The more I read, the more my imagination soared. Here was a mystical system that described my own experience.

Most of all I was fascinated by the tradition of meditation in Jewish mysticism. I hadn't known about it before.

In my years of study, I had had the impression that Jews don't meditate. Such activity seemed unsociable in a religion that is constructed around collective experience. Jewish prayers don't begin unless a minyan—ten men—gather; in less traditional settings, the minyan includes women, but the principle remains. And once the service starts, the prayers are said together, not separately. The only time sanctioned for private meditation in most synagogues is a few moments at the end of the *Amidah,* the one silent prayer.

Yet here in Jewish mysticism was an emphasis on meditation. I was fascinated, as I was discovering within myself the importance of silence. I read avidly about Jewish teachers in past centuries who instructed their students to meditate alone for hours a day, to bring them to a closer connection with the divine. In preparation for certain meditations, these same teachers and students fasted for long periods. Descriptions of their meditations, many of which have come down to us, sounded as full of promise as any I'd read about in the late twentieth century.

In France, and the months that followed, I began to meditate. Breath in. Breath out. Breath in. Breath out. I had done a simple meditation of observing the breath in the past, but it had been a quick fix at anxious times rather than a constant practice, and I always thought of it as an import from another culture, vaguely Buddhist or Hindu.

As I began to meditate after reading about Jewish meditation, I understood that this, too, could be part of a Jewish spiritual practice. I was awkward at first. Sitting for ten or fifteen minutes, I became restless, and my mind wandered. Many days I forgot to do it. But when I came back to that silence within, I felt its power.

* * *

Lighting the candles alone. *Davvening* the Saturday morning service alone. Meditating alone. I thrived on the aloneness. I seemed to be moving deeper and deeper into a spiritual realm.

But what about my connection with the Jewish religious community? I didn't want to drift too far away. During my fallow-field years I had not gone to religious services, but now I decided to try them once again. Perhaps I would find a spiritual base there, as I had before.

One Saturday morning I slipped into a seat in the back of a local conservative synagogue. I had chosen this synagogue because women participated in leading the services, even though the liturgy was traditional. As I began to join in the prayers, I was relieved I could follow the Hebrew after so much time away.

But the prayers were just as male-centered as always, and I was jarred by their frantic pace, rushed through without much feeling. People seemed to be paying more attention to each other than what they were doing. The atmosphere distracted me, and I could not settle into a meditative state. After a while, I got up and left.

I would try the Jewish renewal congregation, I decided. There I might discover what I was looking for, as the God-language of the liturgy is balanced between masculine and feminine. For years I had been associated with the Jewish renewal movement. Even during my withdrawal from religious life, I had stayed active in the progressive secular organizations that are part of it. If any Jewish group was my natural community, Jewish renewal was it.

On a Friday evening I dropped by the Shabbat gathering of the local Jewish renewal congregation, held in a member's home. People were sitting on the floor on big pillows, socializing, and the program had not started, even though the sun had already set.

"Hey, everybody, please be quiet," a woman finally said, an hour later. "I'd like to do some preparation before we light the Shabbat candles. Let's talk about how this last week has been, so that we can let go of it and move into Shabbat."

"You begin," somebody called.

The woman started to describe a problem with her teenage daughter, then she went on at length about an automobile accident she had witnessed. It had brought up serious feelings of depression. I looked around the crowded room, thinking it would take hours for everyone to tell their stories. "Do you do the evening service here?" I whispered to the man next to me.

"I don't know," he answered. "Sometimes, I think. Yes."

My stomach started to growl. The potluck dinner, which apparently came last, would take place around midnight at this rate. I felt like a grouchy child, unhappy that my needs weren't being met. "I don't think I'll stay," I whispered. With that, I slipped out the door.

Later I wondered why I had been so quick to leave. I usually enjoy hearing stories about people's lives. The evening undoubtedly had come together; I had spotted a few members of the congregation in the room who were capable of leading the Shabbat evening service. I might have missed out on a moving experience, as Jewish renewal *davvening* is especially beautiful, with a lot of heartfelt singing.

But it didn't matter. I had learned what I needed to know: I still did not have the patience for Jewish religious services. I was too sensitive, too easily irritated. Although I wanted to be part of a spiritual community, the time was not right. I'd reconnect in the future, but for now my task was to continue alone.

As I experimented with meditation and spent more time by myself, I began to feel the desire to pray every day. I remembered how I had felt among the boulders in France, when I had done the morning Shabbat service. That had been one of the most deeply satisfying spiritual experiences of my life. Was there some way I could bring the same combination of prayer and meditation into my daily life?

Once the question was posed, the answer appeared. Without forethought, I picked up my daily prayer book one morning and made my way through the service. Instead of saying all the words, I took the theme of each section, and prayed or meditated on it. It worked. Just as I had found a deep sense of peace in France, I found it in my own house. I didn't need the crashing waves or the warmth of stone.

Thus I began a spiritual practice that continues even now:

The morning light comes through my bedroom window, and I rise from bed, stretching, aware of my body, giving thanks that I am alive.

I notice the beauty outside, the olive tree in the wind, the bamboo, the little hummingbird, and I contemplate the fullness of this universe.

I focus on the passing of time, reflecting on the morning light that comes after darkness, just as darkness comes after light.

My awareness shifts to the divine love that exists in all life, and I express my gratitude.

The wave of the *Sh'ma* begins to pass through me. I

say the words aloud: *"Sh'ma Israel, Adonoi Eloheinu, Adonoi Ehad."*

As the wave recedes, I name my commitments and responsibilities. This is what I give back to the universe in gratitude for all that I receive.

I enter the most intimate moment, the *Amidah*. I praise God and express whatever is deepest in my heart, my despair, my needs, my hopes, my dreams, and I end with thankfulness.

Finally, I reconnect with community, acknowledging the pain that exists and imagining a world that is healed. As I commit myself to do this work along with others, I say, "Amen."

This, then, is my morning service. Different each day, because I am always changing, but the structure remains the same. Sometimes I stay silent throughout, meditating; other times I sing parts of it and move about, or read the traditional prayers. It is a vessel large enough to contain anything I feel.

As I began to do this service regularly, I noticed I felt calmer and more content. When I didn't have time for it, the day lacked an important dimension. Thirty or forty minutes seemed just about right, in my home, quiet. But I discovered shortcuts. The service could be compressed to a twenty-minute early morning walk, or even a ten-minute shortened version if I was in a hurry to leave the house.

My spiritual life was becoming richer than I had known before. But I had another discovery to make, this one about my relationship to the divine.

When I was very young, God was the father-in-the-sky. Through my church years, until I became an atheist, he remained the wise father. When the divine reappeared in my life that day in 1979 in my psychotherapy office, it was a high, loving presence that had no gender. But as a Jew, who or what was God?

My studies of Kabbalah gave me permission to name the God I knew, the holy presence that infuses all of life. To my relief, I found like-minded thinkers in Kabbalistic history. Isaac Luria, for example, taught in the sixteenth century that the sparks of God exist in all matter, and our task is to help return them to the divine source. A giant healing, a *tikkun,* is imagined, in which God is made whole once again.

The mystical idea of God being present in all of life fits my experience. I welcomed learning that this concept exists within Judaism, even though it is not the dominant view. But how does one have a personal relationship with such an amorphous entity?

As a child, saying my prayers before bed at night, I thought there was a direct line upward into the heavens, and a listening God. But now, as I did the morning service every day in my home, I realized that I could not imagine God's metaphorical ear, even though I was experiencing it.

In Judaism a distance is assumed between the people and God. Sometimes this distance is less, as when praying to Elohim or Shechinah, or it is more, as when praying to Adonoy. But whatever name for God is used, a respectful attitude is always kept. In the *Amidah,* the silent prayer, for example, the traditional Jew takes three steps back, three steps forward, and bows, as one would bow to a ruler. Only then can the prayer begin. And the prayer itself starts with collective blessings and praises, as the appreciation of God must be voiced before anything personal can be added. It concludes with collective thanksgiving.

This relationship to prayer is different from the Christianity of my childhood. Grandma Alice's prayers were very personal. She'd throw her head back, raise her hands, and plea spontaneously for what she wanted. Merging with God seemed to be her everyday experience.

But Jews are careful not to ask for too much, and their requests are voiced in the plural, so that it is the people asking for strength, or peace, or whatever, not the individual. God doesn't respond to presumptuousness, it is understood.

Part of my attraction to Judaism was this distance. No simple clamping on the shoulder, buddy-to-buddy with God here. Or I want this, and I want that. Jewish prayers have been transmitted word for word through the centuries. All these formal prayers and all the names for God help to keep the mystery of the divine intact.

Still, when I began to do the daily morning service in my own way, I found myself talking to God. Not a lot, not like Grandma Alice, but during the *Amidah* I'd speak directly. My words came from the depth of my being, and I had the experience of being seen and heard in a way that was more sensitive, more truthful, more loving than anything I've known with another person. Often I received an amazing understanding, far beyond anything I could have figured out for myself.

My relationship with the divine seemed to be growing more intimate. But what sense could I make of it? Although this holy presence was personal, and "spoke" to me, I did not think of the divine as a God that speaks.

I puzzled over this, wanting my beliefs and my experience to be congruent. But soon I gave up. I could only trust my experience and accept the paradox. As Jews have said for centuries, God is unknowable.

* * *

My earliest lessons about Jewish observance were learned in the orthodox setting. The rules were clear: this is what you do, and this is what you don't do. The lines were carefully drawn. If you had a question, the rabbi or a learned person could be consulted to find the answer.

The system appealed to my desire for order. As a new Jew, it helped keep ambiguity at bay. No wonder that many converts feel most comfortable within orthodoxy.

But I was making Judaism my own. After the fallow-field period, I approached Jewish spirituality with an openness that I didn't have when I was so imbued with orthodoxy. In the past I had felt uncomfortable when all the words of the traditional prayers were not said, but now I allowed myself to experiment with the liturgy itself, choosing what was most relevant to my experience.

I no longer was passive. If I didn't wish to go to synagogue services, I could *davven* and meditate alone. And if the God-language in the traditional liturgy sometimes bothered me, I could change it. Judaism was less static than I had believed.

With this understanding, then, I finished my passage across the Red Sea. It had taken far longer than I expected. But the convert with an attitude was now a Jew who had passed through disappointment and disillusionment, and come to the other side.

Shavuot, 1996

On the holiday of Shavuot, Jews celebrate the revelation of the Torah on Mt. Sinai.

Forty-nine days have elapsed since the beginning of Passover. Each day we've become increasingly open, so that we are now ready to receive the word of God in our own lives, just as it was received by the people at the base of Mt. Sinai thousands of years ago.

Shavuot is a holiday without ritual. Traditionally it is observed by studying Torah throughout the night. This custom comes from the Kabbalistic belief that the heavens open then, so we must stay awake to hear what comes through. Jews gather in homes, synagogues, and public spaces with their blankets and pillows, dressed in jeans or sweats, looking like they've come to a campout. But instead of sleeping, they learn together until dawn.

One year ago on Shavuot I was in Jerusalem. In that intense environment I went from study session to study session. I didn't want to miss anything. But here in my town in California, Jewish life is much less dense, the choices fewer. This year I will settle into the gathering at my nearby community center, content to learn with people I know.

Undoubtedly we will study the biblical book of Ruth, which is read in synagogues on Shavuot. Some years I've been moved by her courage and stamina; other times I've chafed at the image of her perfection. We will also puzzle over the Mt. Sinai experience, teasing out the mystical explanations. What really happened on that mountain, and how does it play itself out in our lives? I've grappled with this question while writing these pages, but I am ready for new insight.

One year, and more, has passed since I began this book. The process of writing has kept me in an introspective state. I've not been able to escape the disturbing questions, the uncomfortable moments. On the surface my story has been about conversion, a woman who yearns to be a Jew, and the ensuing struggle to find spiritual meaning and a place among the Jewish people. But a subtext exists, that of a woman striving to be more fully herself.

As much as I've wanted to reveal the truth of my experience, I've had the impulse to remain concealed. I've caught myself writing descriptions that are too short or hiding my feelings in a flat emotional tone. The old voices accompanied me this year: "Who will be interested? Who cares?" And the hardest: "How dare you speak of these things?"

Each day I look at what I've written, checking to make sure I have been honest. Sliding past the truth happens so easily, a word here or there, leading to a different meaning. My dishonesty, I've learned, comes from self-deception, or a desire to protect myself, or habitual oversight.

I've come to see my life's experience with greater clarity. I am reminded of the Hasidic rabbis who could look into peoples' faces and recognize their largest spiritual task. "You must learn to let go of your envy," it might be said. Or, "You need to open yourself up to the love of God." Whatever the verdict, it required years of meditation and prayer. This was considered holy work, since we help to heal the world by healing ourselves. The process of writing has some of this same quality.

During these months I've been conscious of the passage of time. In Judaism this passage is acknowledged by the daily prayers and the holidays that mark the months and seasons. One moment gives way to the next; nothing stays the same.

When I was in Jerusalem last year, I meditated every morning in a field a few minutes' walk from my apartment. There I sat on a large rock, surrounded by tall grasses and wildflowers, enclosed, safe, yet open to the sky above. The sound of the insects and the birds overhead filled my ears. In the weeks between Passover and Shavuot, the grasses turned from green to yellow, the flowers bloomed then faded.

Before I left Jerusalem, I brought my notebook and pen to this field for one last visit. "My Field," I wrote in big letters at the top of a page, sketching in the folds of land, the rock, the dried grasses and flowers, the pine tree nearby. I wanted to capture all of it, keep it just as it was. Yet tomorrow would be different from today, the earth a little more parched, the color of the vegetation even more yellow. And soon, I heard, this field would be bulldozed to build new houses.

Passover gives way to Shavuot. One year gives way to the next. The passage of time has its own beauty, but I also know its sadness. I am a woman growing older. The wisdom gained through the years, the lessons learned from my mistakes, comfort me, but I cannot deny my mortality.

In the midst of change, Judaism gives us order. It reassures us with its rules and laws, rituals and liturgy. Although we do not know when we will die, we act as though we are in control of our everyday lives.

Sometimes I forget that change is inevitable. It seems that the worst things, especially, will remain the same. I am thinking here about sexism in Judaism. During my years of crossing the Red Sea, I saw it as a permanent fixture, wrecking something I loved. Nothing could be done, because it was so inextricably woven into the religion.

I had to let go of my cynicism before I could return spiritually to Judaism. I had to take the long view, recognizing that change is as much a part of human history as it is of the natural world. Although I most likely will not know a Judaism entirely devoid of sexism in my life, I am heartened by the possibility of this transformation over time.

A shift is already taking place. Over the past two decades, exciting new feminist liturgy and rituals have been created within the Jewish renewal movement. One can't be around Rabbi Zalman, or Rabbi Marcia Prager, or Rabbi Shefa Gold without absorbing a Judaism that is spiritually alive. God is "she," as well as "He," and humans are not "Man," but another species in the grand creation of the universe.

Even within orthodoxy there is change. No longer satisfied with the status quo, modern orthodox women are stretching Jewish law as far as they can, so that they can participate more fully in the religious and communal life of their shuls. As more of these women study Jewish texts, they are becoming teachers and leaders in their own right.

In all the denominations except orthodoxy, women rabbis are now commonplace. A decade ago this was not so. These women spiritual leaders and teachers are helping to create a much-needed balance in a tradition heavy on hierarchical structures and male concepts of God.

Jewish feminists can gain strength from the work of

women in other religions. Sandy Boucher, in her book *Turning the Wheel,* charts the course of American Buddhist women as they strive to integrate feminism into a patriarchal Buddhism. Protestant and Catholic feminists, critical of patriarchal Christian theology, have introduced feminist concepts of God, promoting an earth-based understanding of spirituality. Women everywhere are putting pressure on male-dominated religious structures. These women are our compatriots as we create a Judaism that includes women's understanding.

In my return to Judaism, I looked for guidance to women who seemed able to hold both a love of Judaism and a commitment to feminism. One of these women, Susie Schneider, lives in the Old City in Jerusalem. A scholar of Jewish texts, she leads a quiet, meditative life, lingering longer than anyone I know over each word of the prayers, observing each ritual act with the greatest devotion. Daily her apartment is filled with students who come to learn, and she runs an international correspondence program in Jewish thought and practice. Yet with all this activity, the quiet around her remains.

A feminist in the United States before she emigrated to Israel, Susie is dedicated to educating women and men about the mystical aspects of Judaism. She wants to help them open to the wisdom that lies within the tradition. Her work is done in an orthodox context. For years she has led a traditional orthodox life, experiencing a spiritual depth there that she's not found elsewhere.

When I stayed with Susie in Jerusalem last year during Passover, I admired her commitment to Judaism. She seemed to be conscious of it in every daily act, and she often spoke about the power of the *mitzvot.* I wondered if I could lead such a traditional life, but I knew I couldn't. Although I am drawn to it, my concern about sexism keeps me away from those parts of the tradition that diminish women. Fortunately, a great deal is left, more than I can learn and absorb in this lifetime.

One cold night while I was in Jerusalem, I hurried through the Old City streets to the Western Wall. The hour was late, well after midnight. I expected to see a large crowd, as this was the night of Passover when Jews traditionally sing and dance at the wall, but the large space was almost empty. Even the most hardy must have had second thoughts about going out in the freezing weather.

On the women's side of the wall I drew my fleece jacket around me, protection against the whipping wind. Climbing on a metal chair, I peered across the six-foot barrier to the men's side, where I could see about twenty black-suited young men, illuminated by huge neon lights. They began to hop around in a circle, singing bravely in the cold. As more men arrived at the wall and the circle grew, their voices became stronger, their dancing more vigorous. Most of their melodies were familiar to me, Shlomo Carlebach's songs.

A few other women had come to the wall. At first we didn't pay attention to each other, but then we began to share complaints about the weather, a few words in English, a few in Hebrew.

One of the women reached out her hands, beckoning us to dance together. "Good idea!" I smiled.

"Should we?" another gestured. Beneath her question was centuries of conditioning.

But then we all shrugged. "Why not? It's too cold."

With a leap, we joined together and began to sing along with the men. In our little circle we spun around faster and faster. Soon we were singing our own songs, creating our own rhythms.

In that eerie, freezing night, I was having a new wall experience. I was doing what the men were doing. Always before, I had envied the men praying together, reading from the Torah. We women pray alone at the wall, each with her own prayer book or thoughts, because women are not allowed to lead prayers or read from the Torah in orthodox Judaism. But now, when nobody was watching, we were mirroring the men.

Afterward I thought how sad, how pathetic our situation. I had felt jubilant, but where was the victory? Women singing and dancing together is not prohibited in orthodoxy. If we had tried to enter the men's side and join their circle, we would have been thrown out. Or if we had started to pray together, opening up a Torah, pandemonium would have ensued.

When I read in the Jewish newspaper about Women at the Wall, an international organization that is fighting for women to be allowed to hold services there, I feel despair. Their progress is so slow, the patriarchal control so entrenched.

How do I make my peace with this, and other forms of sexism within the religion and the community? I don't. I carry the image of what can be, and work in my own way to bring it about.

Over time, I trust, the efforts of Women at the Wall will succeed. Despite the stranglehold of the religious right in Israel, change is built into Judaism. Jewish law, *halakhah*, is constantly evolving, although it appears to be static. The effects of the second wave of feminism, and the continuing dissatisfaction of women, are putting pressure on the system, and we will see the results.

It is hard to contain both hope and discouragement about the process of changing patriarchal Judaism. Sometimes I forget the obstacles and become complacent. Other times I become discouraged and feel like giving up. But I trust my commitment to Judaism after all these years. As my spiritual journey continues, I might withdraw once again into a fallow-field state, but I know I will return, as I have before.

I write these words with satisfaction. For a very long time I thought I didn't have the capacity for commitment, except to my children. Changing from one career to another, leaving husbands, I worried that something was wrong with me. I had strayed too far from the life I was supposed to lead, and I didn't have faith in myself.

When my friend Barbara visited me a few years ago, I was at the height of this self-doubt. One afternoon, sitting on a beach along the Pacific Ocean, we spoke about our regrets.

"You've had such an interesting life," she began. "There are so many things I haven't experienced."

"But I admire your stability," I answered. "You've accomplished something I haven't, staying married to the same person for over thirty years, working it out."

"There have been trade-offs."

I sighed. "Always the trade-offs. But don't they seem worth it? You and Stanley have a great relationship."

She was quiet for a few moments. "Yes, but I still envy your adventurousness."

"And I regret that I haven't had a more committed, stable life," I answered.

In the months that followed, I mourned the lack of constancy in my life. Reaching my fifties, I had not been successful in this area. Never would I have the history of one long relationship. I told friends about my feelings of failure, and wrote in my journal about it.

But as I unlocked my sadness, I realized once again

that my relationships have brought great richness to my life. Even now my circle of family extends to include ex-mates, ex-in-laws, and ex-stepchildren.

Each of us has her or his own way of learning commitment. For me, it has come through my struggle with Judaism rather than with one partner. Although my path is unconventional, I have learned what I needed to know. Now I look back, charting the course of my relationship to this religion, seeing the stages of infatuation and disillusionment, and then the unfolding deep commitment. Judaism has taught me what it means to say, "I commit myself for the rest of my life."

In this year of writing, my Jewish spiritual practice has continued to flourish. Now that I have let go of the orthodox idea of doing it in a certain way, I feel free to explore the possibilities.

I have taken on those observances that mean the most to me. Each one has spiritual depth, and together they complement each other. For example, praying for the earth to be healed leads me to commit myself to use the earth's resources with care. I study about the Torah's concern for the land, and then I involve myself in *tikkun olam,* political action, by writing a letter protesting the toxic waste dump nearby. On the holiday of Tu Bishvat, I gather with others in appreciation of the trees, and we share our concerns about their survival.

Central to my spiritual practice is Shabbat. I sometimes spend Friday evenings with Sarah and Jacqueline, my little granddaughters. As their parents go out for the evening, we set the table with the Shabbat candles, special grape juice, and challah. They are not Jewish, but Sarah loves to say the *kiddush* over the grape juice, and Jacqueline pulls apart the challah, giving us each a piece. Together we sing *"Shabbat Shalom"* and say the blessings, and I feel connected once again to the generations before and the generations after.

The newest flowering of my work is at Chochmat HaLev, a center of Jewish spirituality in the San Francisco Bay Area. Here I teach classes and supervise students. Sometimes my insecurity about being a convert returns, but the feeling passes as I remind myself that this work is a gift, and that I have spent years preparing for it.

Often I teach my students about Jewish spiritual practice. It can begin with one small observance, I say, describing that time when I began to reconnect to Judaism by lighting the Shabbat candles. Or I tell them about a secular woman I know who revealed to me that the sound of the *Sh'ma* was the only thing that moved her in Judaism. I suggested she repeat it at night before sleep. A month later she called: "I'm hooked," she said. "I've been saying the *Sh'ma* every night. Can you teach me more?"

My message to my students about Jewish spiritual practice is enthusiastic. I consider such a practice to be full of richness, whether one takes on meditation or prayer, or concentrates on blessings. The list continues: studying Torah, observing Shabbat, doing *tikkun olam,* singing *niggunim,* celebrating the holidays. Each of us can find things here to give our life meaning.

My practice shifts from time to time. Recently I've become unsettled about the issue of food. Orthodox Jews observe *kashrut* because it is mandated by Jewish law, although it makes no logical sense. For them it is a statement of commitment to God. I feel the pull of the tradition, but environmental and ecological issues also concern me, and I care about the life and death of the animals we eat.

The easiest way out of this dilemma is to become a vegetarian. But even that is not so simple, because sometimes I hunger for chicken. Is kosher chicken really more holy than free-range chicken? Is it really crucial that I eat no animal blood? The point for me is to remain conscious of every act, so that I know what I am doing and make the connection with the divine.

In my town several Jewish communities exist. I float between them, depending on my mood. Chochmat HaLev feels most like my spiritual home. On Saturday mornings I sometimes *davven* there. The east wall of the center, two stories high, is made of painted bricks, and it reminds me of the Western Wall in Jerusalem, with its uneven surface. I press up against it to say the *Amidah,* and I am transported thousands of miles away to the Western Wall, remembering those times there when I found strength.

At Chochmat HaLev people come to me for spiritual guidance. Although I often don't have the answers, I draw on my experience. I have more contact with death now, as I am connected to people in the community who are very ill. Realizing that death is as much a birth as life, I am ready for this.

In my life is a new love, a man with whom I sometimes share Shabbat. Once again I am exploring the beauty of intimacy, the terror of connectedness. Am I prepared, finally? I don't know, but I think I am. My experience as a Jew has taught me.

During this year I've struggled once again with the issues of conversion. All the old feelings have come to the surface. I've seen my pettiness, and the way in which I held onto anger. I've learned how my attitude of cynicism and discouragement kept me from growing spiritually. My part in the difficulties has become more apparent. Were I to begin conversion now, I would have a more balanced understanding.

Still, serious problems exist for converts. A great deal of work in the Jewish community remains to be done for us to feel safe and to thrive. Certainly this must take place on the structural level, with conversion proceedings made clearer, and the denominations coming to some accord about what makes a person a Jew. Temples, synagogues, and shuls must find ways to bring converts lovingly and respectfully into the community.

On a more subtle level, the attitude toward converts needs to change. Jewish hostility toward non-Jews is too easily deflected onto us, giving us pain. We should not have to struggle so hard to be accepted or to be considered legitimate. According to Jewish law, we are fully Jewish once we've converted. Although we do not share the same childhood ethnic experience, we share a deep commitment to the Jewish people.

I recently received a call from Richard, a Jewish friend. "I'm afraid something's wrong with me," he said. "The only women I'm interested in are converts, or in the process of converting."

"*Nu?* So?" I answered, mildly offended. "What's the problem?"

"I must be *mishuganah,* crazy," he continued. "I'm a committed Jew."

"So what?" I answered. "It's not shameful to fall in love with a convert. We're Jews, as much as anyone who's been born Jewish."

"Yes, but . . . "

I filled in the spaces. I knew he was thinking about Jewish lineage, Jewish blood, Jewish experience. Even though I was ready to defend converts, I had some sympathy for him. I remembered how the cultural differences between Michael and me caused misunderstanding. It isn't easy to navigate these issues in a relationship.

But I was tired of his chauvinism. "Give it up, Richard," I said. "Stop feeling sorry for yourself. You should feel grateful that a convert wants you, because most of us are very high souls."

He thought about that for a minute. "You're probably right," he said.

In my talks with converts, I've heard too many sad stories. One of the worst was told to me recently by a single mother, a doctor, who has an eight-year-old son. This boy doesn't know his mother is a convert, although he knows his father was an anonymous sperm donor. She has carefully cut the pictures of her first Catholic communion out of her scrapbook and diminished contact with her Christian relatives, so that he will believe she was born Jewish.

"Every night I think I should tell him the truth," she confided sadly. "I want to, but I'm scared."

When I asked about her fear, she answered: "This knowledge will affect his life. He goes to a Jewish day school, and the other kids will treat him differently, once they know. It will never be the same for him again."

"But maybe he won't tell," I said, falling momentarily into the delusion that concealment helps.

"It will get out."

This woman went on to describe her plan. One night, after she reads her son a bedtime story, if he's in a good mood and they are feeling close, she will tenderly say, "I have something to tell you."

I am angry that this woman has to scheme so carefully

and so painfully to find a way to share with her son a fact that should bring both of them pride. The world I envisage would have converts and born-Jews side by side, different but nonetheless equal in our connection to this heritage that roots us all.

Throughout history Judaism has lost Jews and gained Jews. Many have left because of assimilation and conversion to other religions. Others died prematurely because of persecution. This loss in numbers, a tragedy, has been balanced partly by conversion.

I think now of the converts I know, their level of commitment and their understanding, their passion for this religion of their choice. They have great vigor, and they help to keep the religion and culture alive. Is this not at least some consolation for a Jewish people still reeling from the Holocaust and concerned about continuity?

Nehama. The name I took at conversion, meaning comfort and compassion. On first glance it is a simple name, rooted in the earth, receptive, responsive. The divine feminine.

But I know it to be fierce. When I chose this name as my own, I understood that it required an oath of self-preservation. The giver of comfort can be overwhelmed by demands, and the well of compassion can be drained dry.

I would not let my name lead me into passivity. In its fierceness Nehama is also the defender of others. Compassion gives way to speaking out, to protecting those who are in need. Comfort goes beyond reassurance to action.

My name is like me, beginning in the body, the warmth of earth. Then it opens to another realm, that of divine connection.

While writing this memoir, I have had dreams of floating. They have come as a gift, leaving me replenished and restored. Usually I rise to the ceiling in these dreams, feeling great pleasure, but recently I went even higher.

I had the most beautiful vision.

I was outside in a clearing bounded only by trees, standing on rich earth that smelled of spring. Around me people were *davvening,* our prayers led by a woman. The sound of the prayers filled me, a sweet, gentle sound.

I looked up. Above me several people were floating. I knew I could do it, too. Exhaling, I rose in the air, above the leafy branches of the treetops. The *davvening* continued, now a smaller sound.

I was filled with the greatest joy imaginable, greater than I know on this earth. For a while I floated in the endless sky.

But it was time to come down. The voices below let me know. Slowly I brought myself toward the earth. As I descended, I felt myself split open with joy, radiating to the people below.

And then, just before I landed, I began to awaken.

I became aware of the bed, and my pillow, and the daylight coming through my window. Still, the vision remained. I felt that space in the center of my back, just before exhalation, and I knew without a doubt that I would rise to the heights once again.